Praise for *The Digital Helix*

"You can't successfully manage transformations without effectively managing expectations. By ruthlessly confronting how digital innovation explicitly disrupt enterprise expectations, Gale and Aarons focus executive attention exactly where it belongs: the challenge of aligning greater expectations with greater value."

—**Michael Schrage, research fellow at MIT Sloan School's Initiative on the Digital Economy**

"In my role at Forbes Media, I have the good fortune and honor to meet personally with, write about and to conduct research among many hundreds of corporate leaders and entrepreneurs around the globe. Each is to a greater or lesser degree leveraging Welch's dictum and the parallels between those experiences and what I learned from reading *The Digital Helix* are striking."

—**Bruce Rogers, chief insights officer at Forbes**

"Don't let the title fool you; this goes way beyond digital. Gale and Aarons have given us a refreshing perspective about the importance of simplicity, clarity, and culture in any transformation, along with a poignant reminder that we must never lose sight of our most critical asset—the very people we serve."

—**Colette LaForce, named one of the Top 50 Women in Technology, a Fierce 15 CMO, and CMO Leader of the Year**

"Those who can take an adaptive stance, both as individuals and organizations, are best positioned to realize their full potential during uncertain times. Through research and insights, Gale and Aarons provide the approach and tools for executives to lead by example in order to thrive in the digital age."

—**Vanessa Colella, head of Citi Ventures and Chief Innovation Officer, Citi**

"It isn't enough to evolve your existing business processes. Gale and Aarons understand that businesses need real transformation. In *The Digital Helix*, they provide information and tools to help you understand what successful transformations look like."

—**Kelly Faley, Vice President, Digital Marketing, Sharp HealthCare**

THE DIGITAL HELIX

THE DIGITAL HELIX

Transforming Your Organization's
DNA to Thrive in the Digital Age

MICHAEL GALE & CHRIS AARONS

GREENLEAF
BOOK GROUP PRESS

This publication is designed to provide accurate and authoritative information in regard to the subject matter covered. It is sold with the understanding that the publisher and author are not engaged in rendering legal, accounting, or other professional services. If legal advice or other expert assistance is required, the services of a competent professional should be sought.

Published by Greenleaf Book Group Press
Austin, Texas
www.gbgpress.com

Copyright ©2017 Michael Gale and Chris Aarons

All rights reserved.

Thank you for purchasing an authorized edition of this book and for complying with copyright law. No part of this book may be reproduced, store in a retrieval system, or transmit by any means, electronic, mechanical, photocopying, recording, or otherwise, without written permission from the copyright holder.

Distributed by Greenleaf Book Group

For ordering information or special discounts for bulk purchases, please contact Greenleaf Book Group at PO Box 91869, Austin, TX 78709, 512.891.6100.

Design and composition by Greenleaf Book Group and Sheila Parr
Cover design by Greenleaf Book Group and Sheila Parr
Backside jacket artwork by Zach Layton

Cataloging-in-Publication data is available.

Print ISBN: 978-1-62634-992-6

eBook ISBN: 978-1-62634-465-5

Part of the Tree Neutral® program, which offsets the number of trees consumed in the production and printing of this book by taking proactive steps, such as planting trees in direct proportion to the number of trees used: www.treeneutral.com

Printed in the United States of America on acid-free paper

22 23 24 25 26 27   10 9 8 7 6 5 4 3 2 1

Second Edition

*To Lara, Wendi, Sam and Jack, and the kids, thank you
for the support, energy, reviews, and love.*

CONTENTS

Preface xi
Foreword xiii
Introduction: Digital Transformation and the Digital Helix: A Primer 1

PART 1: THE NEW DIGITAL WORLD WE LIVE IN 7
Chapter 1: To Thrive with Digital, You Have to Understand the Past. 9
Chapter 2: Tradition Is the Illusion of Permanence 17

PART 2: HOW DIGITAL THINKING
CHANGES YOUR ACTIONS AND RESULTS 29
Chapter 3: Seven Drivers that Will Help You Escape the Old World 31
Chapter 4: The Tao of Getting Digital Done Right 51
Chapter 5: Diving Deep into the Seven Challenges to Digital Transformation . . . 63
Chapter 6: Small Steps Equal Giant Leaps 89

PART 3: THE DIGITAL FRAMEWORK FOR SUCCESS 103
Chapter 7: The Digital Helix: an Introduction 105
Chapter 8: Executives as Digital Helix Explorers. 113
Chapter 9: Themes and Streams for Insights in the Digital Helix 125
Chapter 10: Customers Have Experiential Portfolios 137
Chapter 11: Marketing and Communications as a Flow. 149
Chapter 12: Sales Are Connected Moments 159
Chapter 13: Everyone Together, All the Time 171
Chapter 14: In the Moment and One Step Ahead Always. 183
Chapter 15: Building Optimal Mindset and Culture 195
Chapter 16: Over The Horizon to a Brave New World, for Some of Us 209
Chapter 17: The Next Steps for You 219

Afterword 223
Acknowledgments 225
Notes 227
Index 235
About the Authors 243

PREFACE

This is the very last page we wrote for the book, but we think it is the first one you should read.

You have probably heard, read, or talked a lot about the idea of digital transformation, both inside and outside of your organization. Like other business and management ideas and terms, digital transformation may feel transient or hip, and you may think it will morph or converge into the general landscape of terms. While the phrase might have different meanings and connotations to you right now, you should recognize that digitally transforming is different from just adopting a digital view or adding digital technologies. This "trend" is now the foundation of how we change our thinking and behavior at the organizational and individual level. This begs the questions, *Why should we care about digital transformation, and why now?*

Answering these questions is critical to digital success. Thriving with digital transformation is about discovering, building, and even recreating the best DNA version of your organization. This requires a robust discussion about where you are and where you can go. It is about seeing how new ideas and processes can work together in a manner that might sound contradictory to many tried and tested historical approaches. It is about harnessing the immense promise and potential of technology by changing how your organization thinks and functions at all levels. It is also about giving customers and digital citizens what they want, even before they know they want it. Ultimately, it is about enabling individuals and organizations to reach their fullest potentials, now and in the future, by behaving and organizing in different ways.

We have all seen and experienced a significant amount of change in business in just the past decade or so. With Web 1.0, we were given the promise of access and speed to existing businesses or even new business models. With Web 2.0, we saw the ability to connect organizational elements together and deliver more. But digital transformation is different. Whether it is Web 3.0, 4.0, or even 5.0, digital transformation enables you to be ready for these changes and many others as they come. It is the engine and the underpinnings that enable us to realize our full potential while providing exponential benefits and value to adjust and win in markets and worlds yet to be defined. Your only barrier is creating the right organizational DNA to unleash and maximize its capabilities.

Digital is here and transforming the world around us in new and faster ways than before. Therefore, we must recognize and embrace these changing moments or we will be overcome and left behind in this new world. The question is, *Are you and your organization set up and equipped to thrive and reach your full potential or possibly even overachieve in the digital age?*

This book is designed to give you the insights, frameworks, and stories to identify where you are and where you need to go. We have also included the tools to architect, design, and build the DNA needed to thrive with digital transformation, no matter where you are today. Enjoy the journey.

FOREWORD

THE END IS NEAR

If you remember nothing else from this book, remember this: The end is near. Now that I have your attention, let me explain. The full quote comes not from some deluded prophet of the impending apocalypse but, rather, from none other than the *capo di tutt'i capi* of Forbes Global 2000 CEOs, Jack Welch, former CEO of GE. Welch says, "When the rate of change outside the company is greater than the rate of change inside, the end is near."

The words, like a catchy song you might randomly hear on your Spotify playlist, began to play in an endless loop in my brain. It gets to the heart of the matter of this book: Digital transformation is both necessary and hard. Please pause for a minute to ask yourself where your business falls in this dialectic.

Yes, "digital transformation" may be one of the most overused buzzwords of all time, but this is one of those rare moments when the hype closely matches reality. For many firms thought to be the leaders of our industrial and information economies, these will be trying times. Many will fail—many more, perhaps, than you think. Consider this: It took Amazon twenty-one years to pass Walmart in market value. It took fourteen years for Tesla to pass GM and seven years for Uber to pass Tesla. That's the power of exponential growth in the digital era. What separates winners from losers? Certainly, leadership plays a central role.

In my role at Forbes Media, I have the good fortune and honor to meet personally with, write about, and conduct research among many hundreds of corporate leaders and entrepreneurs around the globe. Each is, to a greater or lesser degree, leveraging Welch's dictum, and the parallels between those experiences and what I learned from reading *The Digital Helix* are striking.

Two cases in point: John Chambers, the legendary CEO (now Executive Chairman) of Cisco, successfully led the company through what he refers to as "five or six" transformational changes in networking technology that helped him create the vision and culture that would drive Cisco from $70 million in revenue when he took the CEO role to today's nearly $50 billion. His strategy: Identify the transitions in technology early and then lean into the change with all you've got. Much of that strategy took the form of acquisitions, some 180 during his tenure, and Chambers was the master of M&A.

Chambers, who is one of the most personable and humble—yet relentless—CEOs I've ever met, is quick to admit his failures as well (like Flip, which turned out to be a $590 million mistake. Oops!) and says this about transformation, "You've got to think exponentially. Not literally, like we were all trained. We were trained to be 3 to 5 percent better. And then you've got to also think about how you position your company for the market and business transitions coming at you at a faster and faster speed.

"I've been successful in my career when I focused on market transitions, and when a transition occurs, you focus on the transition, not your competitor. If you focus on competitors, you're looking backwards. Sounds easy, but it's really hard to do," says Chambers.

Only three years into his role as CEO of Microsoft, when I met him at the company's Redmond, Washington, campus, Satya Nadella had transformed the company culture to prepare it for a future of what he termed "ubiquitous computing and ambient intelligence," a reference to his strategy to tightly weave Office365, Azure cloud, devices, and artificial intelligence initiatives into one seamless platform. The strategy required the company to break down the silos between business units and to change the culture from what Nadella says was one of "know it all" to "learn it all." Exponential change requires new ways of thinking and leading. Chambers's charisma and Nadella's guru-like persona show us that successful digital transformation is first and foremost about change management and cultural change led by example from the top of the organization.

What's your playbook for managing exponential change? It can't come from expecting that the rate of change will continue at the same pace you have experienced to date. In Tim Urban's brilliantly funny and insightful essay "The AI Revolution," he writes, "[Futurist Ray] Kurzweil points out that his phone is about a millionth the size of, a millionth the price of, and a thousand times more powerful than his MIT computer was forty years ago. Good luck trying to figure out where a comparable future advancement in computing would leave us, let alone one far, far more extreme, since the progress grows exponentially."

In today's digital economy, some organizations succeed by adapting to disruptive threats, moving quickly into new markets, attracting the best talent, and maintaining highly regarded brands. Others struggle. They see market share drain away to upstarts; they respond too slowly to market shifts and suffer employee attrition. They get bogged down in outdated processes and systems.

What separates the winners from the losers in a rapidly changing environment, and why are some enterprises rapidly adopting digitally savvy practices and seeing results while others seem decades behind? The next several years will be shaped by the fourth industrial revolution: a new era brought about by technologies such as the Internet of Things, cognitive computing, artificial intelligence, and robotics. For some companies, the transition between the third and fourth revolution is already under way—while others are just beginning to test the waters.

Recent research from Forbes Insights shows that nearly all (93 percent) of Forbes Global 2000 CEOs are undergoing digital transformation. Yet less than half say that their organizations have the capabilities or skills to navigate the change. Other Forbes research tells us that 69 percent of CEOs globally acknowledge that they are concerned about their ability to handle unknown and unforeseen issues. Much of this concern is due to new technologies: 85 percent of these CEOs also cite concern about integrating automated business processes with artificial intelligence and cognitive processes into their present business models.

As my friend, Forbes colleague, and best-selling author Rich Karlgaard puts it, "Digital technology changes everything. . . . [It] is like a death star. First, it pulls your industry, company and career into its orbit. Then it wipes out your old, tired (but nicely profitable) business model. Then it imposes its own laws on how you must run your business. Transform, or you die. Play by the digital rules, or you die. Not just one time, but again and again."

The timing for this book is especially prescient. Next year represents the fiftieth anniversary of the publication of the seminal book *The Double Helix*, by James D. Watson, half of the Nobel Prize–winning duo of Watson and Francis Crick, who brought the term DNA into our everyday lexicon.

Michael Gale and Chris Aarons have brilliantly morphed the description of the helix structure of how our DNA is designed and replicated into an analogy for the structure of the modern, digital-first organization, and the book you're holding serves as the definitive navigation chart to the treacherous waters of digital transformation. It may also come as no surprise that the forces of change outlined in the book were first brought to light by the Austrian-born economist Joseph Schumpeter. According to Schumpeter, the "gale of creative destruction" describes the "process of industrial mutation that incessantly revolutionizes the economic structure from within, incessantly destroying the old one, incessantly creating a new one." This year marks the seventy-fifth anniversary of the publication of Schumpeter's book *Capitalism, Socialism and Democracy*, where the term *creative destruction* first came to light in 1942.

It's also telling that *The Digital Helix* brings to life through research and real-world anecdotes the seven characteristics of a successful digital organization. According to numerology (not that one believes in such things!), the number seven is the seeker, the thinker, the searcher of truth. The seven doesn't take anything at face value; it is always trying to understand the underlying, hidden truths.

Perhaps your firm is struggling to compete against digital-native upstarts. The good news for you is at that it's not too late to leapfrog the competition and turn size and scale to your advantage. It only takes seven steps.

Bruce Rogers
Chief Insights Officer,
Forbes

INTRODUCTION

DIGITAL TRANSFORMATION AND THE DIGITAL HELIX: A PRIMER

More than 80 percent of organizations are attempting to digitally transform[1] the way they operate in the twenty-first century as they try to take advantage of the digital DNA that drives success in high-growth organizations. Research, however, shows how tough digital transformations can be, with fewer than one in six organizations truly succeeding in their vision. To yield the true promise of digital, organizations must change the fundamentals of how they think, act, and behave. This book is designed to show you the pathways to digital success with insights and practices based on primary research and interviews with digital leaders across commercial and government organizations. At the heart of everything is the Digital Helix framework and its seven components for success. Through the Digital Helix, we offer the intelligence, frameworks, and structures essential for building an effective digital organization that can thrive in today's hyper-competitive world.

People are working harder and putting in longer hours than anytime during the past fifty years. Rarely do any of us start working at eight a.m. or stop at five p.m. Technology has created a near-perfect and level playing field for customers and citizens to want to interact with brands and organizations in their own ways on a 24/7, 365-days-a-year basis.

Technology may have opened this window to the new way of working, but digital transformations now drive the very underpinnings of how organizations restructure themselves to handle, manage, and hopefully thrive in this new world. In fact, digital transformations are now the engines to deliver startup-like agility to more established organizations. This book seeks to handle a deeper understanding of what the DNA for successful digital transformation looks like. It does not explore the technologies you might apply to help drive your digital transformation, especially because there is no one-size-fits-all approach. It is designed to give you the best opportunity to be successful by explaining the questions, insights, interactions, behaviors, and triggers that are driving performance for organizations digitally transforming themselves to thrive in this digital-first world. Developing these skills at the individual and organizational levels requires a new way of thinking through challenges and opportunities.

> "We would not be discussing digital transformation with the intensity, fever, or bandwidth that we are were it not for the fact that digital represents and offers a completely different portfolio of economics. Digital makes the expensive cheap and changes the time-consuming to real time. For me, digital transformation is a technical phrase or label for what is really an economic transformation. We are interested in digital because its economics are different from the physical and different from the analog."
>
> **—Michael Schrage, research fellow at MIT Sloan School's Initiative on the Digital Economy, oversees research on digital experimentation and network effects, and is author of *The Innovator's Hypothesis***

To help you get a better handle on the what, the why, and most importantly, the how of digital transformation, we have split this book into three parts:

- An overview of the digital landscape with identification of challenges and drivers
- The new thinking and the Digital Helix framework to help you drive successful transformations

- A discussion of the right processes, mindset, and culture that are imperative for thriving with digital transformation

The first part of this book covers the underlying tensions and opportunities presented by a world rapidly becoming digital. Rather than focus on infrastructure, this section is about the experiences we need to solve problems in this new digital world. A large portion of this section helps break down the challenges and drivers of digital transformation. Our research and experience have shown that identifying the drivers and overcoming the challenges is a key differentiator in truly achieving digital results.

The second part, and main bulk of the book, takes a detailed look at how digital leaders and winners are using new thinking, behavior, and measurement to act in new ways. A cornerstone of this approach is using a new framework we have titled the Digital Helix. It integrates all parts of the organization across sales, marketing, communications, product design, customer service, and human resources to make digital transformation far better than the sum of its parts. This comprehensive structure provides the perspectives and tools needed to use digital to outmaneuver the competition across seven key areas that will transform the business:

1. Leveraging leadership's daily role as an explorer
2. Using digital to inform the organization and help listen in new dimensions for ideas and feedback
3. Understanding that customers have connected portfolios of experiences that drive a different compass for how we respond and interact as an organization
4. Using marketing and communications as two conjoined functions to deliver real value across each customer touch point
5. Transitioning sales from simple relationship or transactional selling to focus on the key moments that matter to your customers
6. Focusing on how all parts of the digital organization need to interact and work together to fuel every customer interaction with insights and in turn make the organization smarter
7. Using all digital information and insights to simultaneously build better experiences and products

The work world of digitally transformed organizations should feel exciting and intriguing because these organizations will become the platforms for future organizations. The more we talked and worked with these digital leaders, the more energized and optimistic they were about the possibilities.

> "The delightful part about digital is that if done right, it actually gets people to tell us who they are and what they're looking for. Organizations can get an actual understanding of what their needs or aspirations are, enabling every business to be much more relevant in their engagement with customers. When that starts to happen, people get excited because you actually see the people you're trying to reach and serve as they are. And it makes a huge difference. But for this to happen, the rate and pace of the adoption of digital for everyone has to happen quickly and in the right way to act on and harness this new power. Principally, most organizations have a skills and mindset gap with the amount of process change, tooling, and data that is being put into place. I'm convinced that the future of digital is going to change so many things. And we can't wait. Most people are just as anxious as I am to get to that future."
>
> —**Jon Iwata, senior vice president, marketing and communications, IBM**

Finally, in the third section of the book we look at three interesting components for highly successful organizations undergoing the digital transformation process:

1. The optimal mindset for delivering high performance in any organization
2. The cultural imperatives for a very different corporate world
3. The future state of Digital Helix organizations

A discussion about how to get each employee to have the right mindset skills to handle this new, digitally transformed world might sound out of context for a business book. However, as Michael Schrage told us, digitally transformed organizations are fundamentally different from their forebears. Digitally transformed organizations, even those in government, rely increasingly on the skills, mindsets, and cultures of their organizations to define success. Technology is abundant everywhere and capital is generally available at low costs, so tried-and-true growth options no longer can be the only way to drive success. Given the speed and effectiveness of how digitally transformed organizations work, we need to enable people to develop specific and different skill sets. Being more flexible with purpose and managing new and constantly changing information creates pressures not unlike those professional athletes confront. Our research and extensive interviews with executives and senior practitioners in the digital transformation process revealed that digital leaders think differently about high performance. In successful digital organizations, pushing the performance envelope, rewarding high performance, and learning how to invest in "optimal" mindsets are all critical parts needed to drive and sustain digital changes.

> "Overall, starting with a feeling of optimism promotes hope and overrides any other sentiments in your work. What would happen if all your employees felt different about coming to work? There would be a different buzz about the building. There would be a different outlook that would help people look forward to what's next and what's coming up. This optimism and hope creates an environment that inspires people to seek out their best and find levels of performance that maybe before they never thought were attainable. Starting with this whole new and different chemistry, any workplace is far better suited to achieve its goals and be its best, even in times of difficulty or adversity."
> —**Pete Carroll, head coach, the Super Bowl Champion Seattle Seahawks**

The final piece of this section looks at the future state of the Digital Helix organization ten to twenty years from now. As we have seen, digital is moving fast and changing organizations rapidly. Leaders must not only recognize the steps and actions they need to take now to thrive with digital, but they must also be able to see and adapt to what the future holds for this dynamic world we live in.

Throughout this book, we have provided research, insights, interviews, and perspectives to help frame the topics and issues and to provide the tools needed to aid you and your organization in delivering real results with digital. We have also added numerous charts, frameworks, and guides to visually show the key elements of digital transformation. The insights shared throughout this book will help you navigate the process of shifting from being just a business doing digital to becoming a true successful digital business now and in the future.

PART 1

THE NEW DIGITAL WORLD WE LIVE IN

CHAPTER 1

TO THRIVE WITH DIGITAL, YOU HAVE TO UNDERSTAND THE PAST AND LOOK TO THE FUTURE

"It is a paradoxical but profoundly true and important principle of life that the most likely way to reach a goal is to be aiming not at that goal itself but at some more ambitious goal beyond it."
—Arnold Toynbee

Though Toynbee had this revelation well over a century ago, this same sentiment could apply to how most executives view the opportunities in the age of digital transformation that we live in now. The nature of digital transformation is pervasive, with more than eight in ten executives focusing their organizations toward its promise.[1] Yet far fewer of them are able to define what the term "digital transformation" means. Maybe the same was true during the Industrial Revolution when humans tried to define what they were experiencing.

In reality, revolutions are often poorly understood until they touch many people or some defining model explains the what, the why, and most importantly, the how. There is significant evidence that many leaders are now trying to ramp up digital transformations in their organizations. In fact, the term "digital transformation" is now a common banner that organizational leaders stand beneath when trying to rally the troops or investors. Many times, their approach is little more than project-focused attempts at digital marketing, using technology to improve business outcomes, or changing an isolated ecosystem in an organization. You may be experiencing similar efforts in your own organization, with digital being touted to improve sales, marketing, customer retention, internal communications, real-time feedback, and more. These attempts are usually not true digital transformations. They are at best business improvements that fall far short of using digital to transform how your organization functions and of delivering future value to your customers.

> "We're trying to be both digital on the outside as well as digital on the inside and focus our investments on what the member will experience. We're being very intentional about how we make the right investments to digitize our business, to drive a digital transformation that manages the benefit to both our members and our internal teams that support them. Our ability to deliver exceptional, differentiated, highly personalized experiences to our members will be as much about how digital we are on the back end as it is on what the members can see and do on the front end."
> —**Chris Cox, head, Digital Experience Delivery, USAA**

Research, both ours and others', shows that the vast majority of organizations that are blazing ahead without a clear road map for success are experiencing suboptimal results from their investments as they go through their own digital transformation journeys. In fact, the basic challenges and the underlying assumptions about our businesses in this digital-first era are fundamentally changing. These changes are as profound as the Industrial Revolution that changed the world some 270 years ago. Like then, there will be a few Luddites who resist the shift. Those who choose not to move forward will ultimately fall by the wayside.

"In my professional experience, the most useful way of thinking about digital transformation is that the economics of digital technologies and platforms become the organizing principle around which business model and business process as well as value creation decisions get made."

—**Michael Schrage, research fellow at MIT Sloan School's Initiative on the Digital Economy, oversees research on digital experimentation and network effects, and is author of** *The Innovator's Hypothesis*

The speed of change, the volume of insights, and the capacity to disrupt market and organization economic models in a few moments are more extreme than at any time before. If Adam Smith, the father of economics and author of *An Inquiry into the Nature and Causes of the Wealth of Nations*, could observe the digital transformations we are undergoing now, one wonders how he would redefine the invisible hand of market dynamics. These dynamics are enabled not just through labor cost reduction but also by digital innovations that are transforming the way we listen, design, deliver, and interact with each other and our customers. Amazon Machine Learning, Omniture, and Salesforce are all living examples of digital transformation systems today.

If you think digital doesn't have the potential to change business, you have not been looking around. There are examples, both large and small, from all over the planet where digital revolutions are changing markets and opportunities. One of the best examples is a program in Uganda called Afri-Gal Tech, which is run by four young women who are trying to improve the process of diagnosing sickle cell anemia, an ailment that kills 80 percent of those afflicted with the disease before they reach the age of five. In most parts of the world, this disease is manageable, but in Uganda, too few hospitals (only three hundred for 37.8 million people within seventy-seven million square miles) and the prohibitive cost of testing make it deadly. By using cell phones with small and inexpensive cameras to diagnose the disease at the touch of a button, these young women have found an easy and cost-effective solution.

This example shows the power of the digital transformation we are living in. Not only does it change the way we think, act, and collaborate, but it will also intensify both opportunities and threats we will face from competitors. If four young women in Uganda can solve a deadly problem by using inexpensive digital technology, then digital transformation being done by small and large businesses across the globe surely can drastically change every facet of marketing, communications, sales, product development, and customer service in more ways than we can imagine.

Almost all the evidence and research we have seen and done ourselves shows how digital transformation too often focuses on only a few initiatives and lacks ambition to go beyond the mere goal of doing something digital. In fact, most organizations miss the mark of becoming truly digital in nature and thus fail to deliver the benefits promised. Yes, organizations need to start somewhere. But digital, if done correctly and in a prevalent way, can not only deliver the benefits expected but also exponentially change the "art of the possible" for businesses and consumers. Now is the time to grab on to the right digital opportunities or risk playing catch-up with the new digital leaders later.

What can organizations do to be digital and gain real competitive advantages? To thrive now and in the future, everyone in the organization has to realize that bringing about a digital revolution in your world requires much more than only taking small steps. Organizations need to focus on a set of principles and practices that underlie the nature of that change.

We saw a similar phenomenon when we first researched how to win with social technology and created the Social Media Accelerator with the Economist Intelligence Unit in 2012 to pinpoint the best practices of leaders. Digging in deeper and looking through 170-plus variables and more than a thousand case studies in our social research showed some distinctive patterns. These patterns clarified how some succeeded while others did not.

> "Social is a catalyst for digital transformation in that the rest of the world is becoming increasingly social, and because of those social interactions, is putting demands on companies to go through a digital transformation."
> **—Charlene Li, principal analyst, Altimeter, a Prophet company**

The Social Media Accelerator research showed that more than 85 percent of Fortune-level executives believe in the potential power of social engagement. But as with digital transformation, barely 14 percent (whom we termed "Thrivers") were garnering any form of real economic returns. This lack of result includes not seeing gains in key variables, such as managing and recruiting human capital, sales, margins, new product development, and even much softer variables such as brand equity. After another wave of social research in 2013 with three times as many respondents, we saw the Thrivers category marginally grow from 14 percent to 16 percent.

All our research projects have shown that the Thrivers were achieving transformative success because they understood the nature of digital and found a way to architect for success. Interestingly enough, these organizations were relatively evenly spread across all segments and sectors, including both regulated and nonregulated industries, as well as manufacturing, retail, health care, and both B2C and B2B. This clearly shows us that success is not driven by industry, but by you and your organization.

To that end, this book isn't a rallying cry for digital transformation. Most organizations understand why they need to be digital or move beyond one or two isolated digital transformation projects to become a fully digitally transformed business. Rather, the data and extensive work in the field show that most organizations simply need frameworks to guide them toward winning with digital now. Thus, we have chosen to focus on this deeper approach, and we view this book as the keystone of an integrated support system that will show you not only why but also how to leverage the delivery of digital transformation to achieve greater results for your organization.

To succeed, leaders need to make sure all their digital investments work together and deliver value that is measurable and greater than the sum of their parts. This phrase, "greater than the sum of their parts," is one we will use often, as it describes the true exponential value you should seek from your digital transformation efforts. Not viewing your efforts this way usually leads to the worst failure in digital transformation, investing in isolation (for example, adding Salesforce or similar digital solutions, but not changing other dependent areas in the organization that could and should be connected to that investment). Investing in isolation defocuses the organization and usually leads to chasing what is next rather than elevating the organization to the task of using digital to solve customer problems and act competitively.

Connecting these investments is vital and cannot be understated. Adam Smith's pin theory, the division of labor, showed that the focused division of connected labor in one system was far more powerful than the same sum of individual craftsmen working in one place, each trying to make the same product. As in the Industrial Age, the Age of Digital Transformation needs a framework for defining and driving success through key functions and roles inside the corporation. Organizations need to understand how people and teams working together in an interdependent way with the tools and information needed is the only way to win as you go through the journey to full digital transformation.

> "Digital transformation requires that we change the way technology organizations connect with the rest of the enterprise. We can no longer think of the technology organization as if it were an arms-length contractor, separate from something called 'the business.' On the contrary, we have to imagine IT and the rest of the business as a single organism, developing hypotheses together, experimenting together, and learning together."
> —**Mark Schwartz, chief information officer, US Citizenship and Immigration Services**

Do Not Fall into the Trap of Digital Wrapping

Digital today is much like the green revolutions of the past decade. Many companies jumped on the bandwagon to make products, services, and businesses that were environmentally friendly, or "green." In truth, most of the initial work by brands in this area was cynically seen as "greenwashing" (when a company or organization spends more time and money claiming to be "green" through advertising and marketing than implementing business practices that minimize environmental impact). Brands such as Ecolab, Whole Foods, and others that are truly green from the ground up paved the way for a genuine recognition across industries of the attainable premium to be found and the need for companies to deliver portfolios of new products and services as consumers became more environmentally conscious. We are seeing the same phenomenon with digital transformation today.

> "This is a vulgar example of digital done wrong when an organization gives their sales team an iPad to interact with customers. This kind of thinking completely misses the point. All these types of things that add digital flavor, digital spice, or a digital emphasis, without organizing, cohering, uniting, or building congruent digitally oriented strategy are bound to fail."
> —**Michael Schrage, research fellow at MIT Sloan School's Initiative on the Digital Economy, oversees research on digital experimentation and network effects, and is author of** *The Innovator's Hypothesis*

Thriving Requires Digital Transformation to Deliver Value Far Greater Than the Sum of Its Parts

Digital should allow all of us to have a far more fluid and real-time approach to market opportunities, as well as to human capital, innovation, marketing, communication, and selling. The fluidity of digital should even extend to new product development and governmental services. The key is effectively tying these areas together and at the same time delivering a more ambitious view of the world. We cannot use a checkbook to buy our way successfully through the digital landscape. Successful organizations understand the need to continuously architect for digital in new, innovative ways.

This new structure also requires a different way of thinking about how we apply our resources. Great companies, like great nations, understand that transformation needs not only change their resource allocation but should also impact architecture, attitudes, mindsets, and the habits of the people and the organization. These aspects are often the most challenging to change because individual and group dynamics slow or impede the progress. As Jim Collins, author of *Good to Great: Why Some Companies Make the Leap . . . and Others Don't*, states, "Greatness is not a function of circumstance. Greatness, it turns out, is largely a matter of conscious choice and discipline."[2] This is true for digital transformation.

From the lowest to the highest levels of organizations, there is interest, passion, and desire for digital transformation. In the vast majority of cases, the missing piece is having a practical framework and playbook for putting it all together and getting it right. Although we do not pretend this book is the pin theory for the Digital Age, the interviews, research, frameworks, and other tools provided will enable you to be far more like the 16 percent of Thrivers who are on the right path toward digital transformation than the majority who are struggling.

Each section of the book will give you the information needed to promote the right thinking internally. The chapters will also provide you with the frameworks needed to identify how to do digital right in your organization. Together, using the digital transformation field guides and the seven key components, which we call the Digital Helix, we will describe and illustrate the solid building blocks that will be the most useful on your journey to do digital right. Now, begin to think about what part of your past can help you learn what it takes to succeed and thrive with digital transformation.

To further help you in the process, we will be augmenting the book with a set of Web tools and digital versions of the field guides on our website. To keep up and begin taking your first steps toward thriving now with digital transformation, please visit our website and ongoing blog at TheDigitalHelix.com.

CHAPTER 2

TRADITION IS THE ILLUSION OF PERMANENCE

"There is nothing more difficult to take in hand, more perilous to conduct, or more uncertain in its success, than to take the lead in the introduction of a new order of things."
—*Niccolò Machiavelli*, The Prince

In 1760, China was the largest economy because for centuries the world was dominated by agrarian practices. Within thirty years, Great Britain became the largest economy. With a population of eight million, Great Britain was about a fourth as large as China, yet it became infinitely more relevant and dominant in such a short time. Something radical occurred for this shift to happen—the Industrial Revolution. Take a moment and think about your organization as it is right now. Is it built more like the old China, where size and traditional market presence mattered, or is it similar to Great Britain, a feisty and unusual upstart unafraid to push new boundaries?

"And both Britain and the world knew that the Industrial Revolution . . . by and through, the traders and entrepreneurs, whose only law was to buy in the cheapest market and sell without restriction in the dearest, was transforming the world.

Nothing could stand in its way. The gods and kings of the past were powerless before the businessmen and steam-engines of the present."[1]

—Eric Hobsbawm, author of *The Age of Revolution*

Most leaders would agree that the digital era we are now in is the start of the next Industrial Revolution and has the power to transform economic markets and even reorganize the brands and organizations we manage. Like the steam engine, spinning jenny, and other advancements that triggered the differing cadence and velocity of each stage of the Industrial Revolution, we have to recognize that Web 1.0, Web 2.0, and the growing economy around the Internet of Things are set to bring upheaval to this version of the industrial and increasingly digital age. You might find this comparison to be ludicrous or even extreme in nature. But the fact remains that now is the time not only to get a jump on the digital revolution but also to identify how your organization can succeed in the long term.

The traditional definition of an economic revolution is rapid, sustained, and significant elevation in productivity, consumption, and economic growth. These economic elements spread across borders and change the nature of trade and even the constructs of national security as they holistically alter business, technology, and even personal landscapes of the time. Think about this definition and what you are seeing now at both market and organizational levels in your market as well as in the world economy.

Across the board, massive changes in technology are changing the nature of trade and how we live and play every day. Although there are similarities between the Digital and Industrial Revolutions, the current version of this new Digital Revolution will not take thirty years. This revolution is already producing radical shifts in business and starting to create new winners, often in less than a few years. Take for example the fashion industry, where designs can be shown and tested not just on the runway but also with real-time social feedback from around the globe. Dresses can now be custom ordered via the Web and delivered in hours instead of weeks to virtually anywhere in the world. Mass customization combined with almost complete compression of supply and demand is creating a totally different growth dynamic for new companies and designers that can break the monopolies of far older traditional brands. This type of phenomenon is happening in almost every industry.

Digital Transformation Perspectives

What's driving marketers and product managers who are really trying to figure out how to serve their customers? It is mass customization. The problem is most brands still don't truly think about the back end and the implications on the manufacturing floor to make it profitable. To get the process right, they need a thoughtful and well-designed system from customer insights through the supply chain all the way to the factory itself. Each aspect of the supply chain must be tied together with technology to keep it running smoothly.

So how much of this is systems, people, and processes? The best brands have a combination of digital, creating the pipes to get information to the factory efficiently, on demand, and in real time. These companies also have the analog for setting up the supply chain in the factory itself in a new way that produces differently so that they can profitably run a high-variable, high-variety product and respond quickly no matter the demand. Half of Nike.com's total revenue per day right now comes from customized product sales, according to Jud Barr, president of JTB Consulting, who works with numerous leading manufacturers on sales, operations, and mass customization. Nike expects customization to be a $1 billion business. As Jud says, "The marketplace has changed with digital. Customers want quick responses, fast delivery, and almost endless choice that includes being able to tailor the product to meet their specific needs. These new digital customers don't want to buy a homogenous product that everybody else has. And we are only in the early stages of this mass customization. Right now, it's still really about decoration, where the customer can choose colors and personalize it. But we're quickly moving into a new era where almost anyone can create products and serve them up in a way that allows the customer to functionally 'build' what they want and adjust specific features so that it suits their exact application."

With new examples occurring daily, this revolution is taking full shape. Leaders are moving toward digital while struggling to understand its direction and potential impact to their businesses. The call to action for most is to make things digital and help their organizations reap the benefits. However, recent surveys show less than 20 percent of leaders can explain or show what digital really means. Most have attempted to do digital—anything via software purchases, technology transformations, marketing experiments, or just plain tinkering. The results have been predictable; there are a few winners with real results and many others struggling to figure out how to take advantage of the magnitude of changes we see in the world. No matter the function—executive, marketing, product development, sales, communications, customer service, support, design, or any other—there is no natural progression here where most organizations would be able to see real results that transform the business or the market.

> "It's not the traditional competitors who worry us. It's the new ones we don't even know about who force us to keep looking ahead. Digital innovation can turn an entire industry on its ear virtually overnight, so it's critical to keep pace. There's no more entitlement of any kind because of company heritage or brand loyalty. Digital capabilities have changed everything about how consumers want to engage with businesses, in both B-to-C and B-to-B. Companies that survive will continue to prove themselves every day to consumers. That's the challenge, and the opportunity, that digital brings. We've got to continue to weave digital into everything we do, to stay ahead of competitors and to serve clients in new, innovative, and creative ways."
> —**Mona Charif, senior vice president and chief marketing officer, NTT DATA Services**

To get the gains that most see as possible and stay ahead of your competition, you must change the way you think about your business and about digital within your organization. Yes, getting 5 percent, 10 percent, or even 15 percent positive change within a function is great. But if the organization is not reimagined, you wind up with slices of improvements that tend to show more problems to be chased rather than truly transforming the business and moving toward the right solution. With the business chasing these problems, the organization becomes defocused and pushes you farther away from what is possible with digital transformation.

Without a full digital transformation strategy in place, organizations are doomed to repeat the mistakes of the past. In the Industrial Revolution, many tried to add steam engines to sailing ships with the expectation that they would deliver comparable benefits to a purpose-built steamship. For a while this was true, but eventually these ships could not deliver because they were neither engineered for the new speed requirements nor had the storage capacity of ships designed to use steam to transform shipping. Steamships have existed since 1813, yet by 1849, the clipper ship was essentially dead. With the opening of the Suez Canal came the need for vastly superior load-carrying, range, and speed capabilities to open new markets. Doesn't that sound like the Digital Age we live in now with mobile, the Internet of Things, customer personalization, and other digital advances?

> "A company that gets digital right is a company built for the future."
>
> —Jon Iwata, senior vice president, marketing and communications, IBM

The owners of sailing ships who put steam engines into their adjusted wooden hulls made the mistake of attempting to bridge the gap rather than transform the whole. History has shown us time and time again that a complete transformation is essential to getting the results needed and to provide the potential to win in the new age. Many shipping companies recognized the need for full transformation and have succeeded. Those that did not failed and went away. As Charles Darwin once said, "It is not the strongest or the most intelligent who will survive, but those who can best manage change."

Volume and Choice Change the Dynamics

Traditional leaders must change the way they contextualize the world. Current market share may still be one of the strongest indicators of brand strength even in an age of digital transformation. However, the capacity to adjust and adapt may end up being a far better metric as the world changes fundamentally around us. Think of it this way: Between 1955 and 2011, 87 percent of companies previously categorized as Fortune 500 went out of business. Giants come and go, and now this process is going to happen even faster. In 1958, the average lifespan of a company on the *Forbes* rankings was more than fifty-five years. It is estimated that by 2018 this average will drop to fewer than fifteen years. Many of the new entrants on the *Forbes* list for 2020 and beyond are being created right now. Imagine how vulnerable your brand could be if a competitor, or perhaps a new company, was able to leverage all the benefits that digital transformation provides twice as fast as you could.

"Digital first" is the new lens for success and how we should view opportunities or threats presented. The profusion of choice will and has changed the way people think, what they will and will not tolerate, and how they make decisions—not just as consumers, but as businesses, workers, and parents. Consider some of these facts as you build your own twenty-first-century versions of steamships for digital transformation:

Everyday Interactions Are Now Increasingly Digital

- 73 percent of job applications are successfully filled through the uses of social media.[2]
- 61 percent of Internet users regularly bank online, and 35 percent of cell phone owners use mobile banking.[3]
- 95 percent of people in a recent survey say they plan to use business communication tools instead of in-person meetings.[4]
- 39 percent of people spend more time socializing on social media than they do face-to-face.[5]

E-commerce Will Continue to Grow and Shape Markets for all Sectors

- 90 percent of e-commerce transactions are business to business (B2B).[6]
- Approximately 23 percent of disposable income worldwide is spent online.[7]

- 80 percent of life insurance purchases start online, and 16.4 million people compare plans and/or sign up on healthcare.gov.[8]

Digital Drives Conversations, Opinions, and Perceptions

- 40 percent of consumers want more digital interactions than companies are providing.[9]
- 53 percent of users recommend companies and products on Twitter.[10]
- 15 percent increase in the churn rate can result from failure to respond via social channels.[11]
- 59 percent of twenty-five- to thirty-four-year-olds discuss poor customer experiences online.[12]
- 81 percent of purchasers get advice from their social networks.[13]

We Are Becoming More Mobile Every Day

- 10 percent of Americans have a smartphone but no Internet at home.[14]
- 92 percent growth in mobile usage occurred from 2013 to 2014.[15]
- 17.4 percent of all Internet traffic is global mobile traffic,[16] which surpassed traditional desktop Internet use in 2015.[17]
- A 100 percent increase in the sales of wearable devices has occurred month after month since October 2012 and has increased exponentially with the launch of the Apple Watch.[18]
- Typical mobile users check their devices more than 150 times a day and spend more than 141 minutes on their devices each day.[19]

The Future Is Being Written and Changed Right in Front of Us

- Content on the Internet tripled between 2010 and 2013.[20]
- There are 1.17 billion unique Google searches each month.[21]
- 16 to 20 percent of Google search queries asked each day have never been asked before.[22]
- An estimated three hundred hours of new video are uploaded to YouTube *every minute*.[23]
- Five million new images are uploaded to Instagram every day.[24]

These stats show that digital is helping to increase the rate and pace of change and creating different worlds for businesses, organizations, and governments. But the world is also changing for the customers and people we serve. You have undoubtedly heard a number of experts proclaiming, "The customer is in control." However, many leaders only look at the customer from a surface perspective. Customers can get what they want, and they are communicating their desires in more abundant and highly personalized ways. They are also reshaping their own experiences while being presented more information than they will ever be capable of digesting. The world that consumers exist in has continued to evolve to a place where there are too many choices to make, both for consumers and for all of us who communicate with them.

> "Technology is transforming innovation at its core, empowering companies to test new ideas at speeds and prices unimaginable even a decade ago. You can stick features on websites and tell within hours how customers respond. You can see results from in-store promotions or efforts to boost process productivity almost as fast. The result? Innovation initiatives that used to take months and megabucks to coordinate and launch can often be started in seconds for cents. That makes innovation, the lifeblood of growth, more efficient and cheaper. Technology makes innovation

agile. Companies are able to get a much better idea of how their customers behave and what they want. This gives new offerings and marketing efforts a better shot at success."

—**Michael Schrage, research fellow at MIT Sloan School's Initiative on the Digital Economy, oversees research on digital experimentation and network effects, and is author of** *The Innovator's Hypothesis*

Digital Transformation Perspectives

Do you think the amount of choice consumers face is hyperbole? Here are the facts: Consumers on average make seventy choices a day[25] and see well over thirteen thousand brand messages[26] (up from five thousand just a few years ago). Tried buying toothpaste recently? If you want to buy Crest, there are twenty-seven varieties alone. Add in Colgate and there are over fifty, and 352 distinct types or sizes of toothpastes are sold retail. This is just one category out of fifty thousand products sold in a typical drugstore.[27]

Providing endless options for everyone is neither possible nor the solution. Rather, the secret is to enable customers to choose what they want with smart digital customization. Look at how Uber, Salesforce, Tesla, Netflix, Amazon (especially Amazon Web Services), and others have seemingly overnight replaced business models or used digital to be efficient and effective and solve customer issues faster and better than traditional leaders. These brands are built around the philosophy of increasing customer success in a digital-first world.

"The aim of marketing is to know and understand the customer so well that the product or service fits him and sells itself."[28]
—**Peter Drucker, author and consultant**

Part of the reason for not getting digital faster is that organizations are focused on measuring success from a historical viewpoint. Watching sales through tracking data, monitoring brand performance, or even getting social feedback drives businesses to improve what they measure. Infinite choices on the consumer side need to be matched with real-time feedback and response on the business side. We would argue that some of the infinite choice comes as a result of poor understanding of the consumer because of reliance on historical data. Do Colgate and Crest really need more than fifty varieties of toothpaste between them? All success stories in digital to date rely on a simple premise: Automate the mundane and enable customers to get what they want in an easy and simple way. This is digital in a nutshell, and given the right tools, insights, and content, customers will solve their issues quickly and without much handholding.

The solution sounds simple: Use digital to better understand your customers. Right? Wrong. There is more to thriving with digital than merely understanding your customers. You need to know where customers want to go—not just where they are right now—and deliver better than the competition. Take Uber for example. Uber is not a digital success story because it is merely a different type of cab company. It wins because it is a digital transportation company that solves a transportation problem that cab companies solve now, but in an elevated manner. The subtlety of this difference cannot be understated. New winners reimagine the problem the customer needs to solve and use digital to make it easy in wonderful and new ways.

Going back to the steamship example, think about the possibilities when you aren't constrained by wind. You find that there are any number of new possibilities and benefits, both small and large, that can stem from moving cargo on the sea with independent power. Uber did not start its business by answering the problem: How do we make cabs more digital? If it did, it would have become a smartphone app tied to a legacy infrastructure. The result would have been a marginal improvement hampered by old technology with little or no differentiation. Instead, Uber started out using digital to turn a travel headache into a luxury experience. Thus, the trick is not to be more digital. It is to *become* digital and use the technology to transform the organization's view of how to solve customer problems. See the difference?

Digital Transformation Perspectives

Uber is not in the taxi business, at least not in the conventional sense, because it owns no cabs and has no cab drivers as employees. Instead, it plays the role of matchmaker, matching a driver/car with a customer looking for a ride and taking a slice of the fare for providing the service. Its value comes from its pricing/payment system (where customers choose the level of service, ranging from a car to an SUV, are quoted a fare, and pay Uber) and its convenience (where you can track the car that is coming to pick you up on your phone screen).

Uber now has newer competitors fighting to take away share. Beyond the "traditional" Uber competitors such as Lyft, there are now companies like Zoox, which recently raised $1.55 billion to tackle mobility and change the way we get around. Even the new darlings of the digital economy are not safe from forward thinking and customer-centric newer digital organizations.

> "At Zoox what we're creating . . . is not a self-driving car any more than the automobile is a horseless carriage. We're not building a robo-taxi service. We're actually creating an advanced mobility service. You can really think of it as Disneyland on the streets of, perhaps, San Francisco, and that means a vehicle that is smart enough to understand its environment, but it's also, importantly, smart enough to understand you, where you need to be, what you want to do in the vehicle, and how you want to move around the city."[29]
>
> —Tim Kentley-Klay, founder, Zoox

Our research, interviews, and experience all point to one key question: How do we take the business foundation we have and combine it with the digital perspective we need to view and solve the problem that customers have? Although all of this may have you worried (and it should), certain fundamental truths don't change and cannot and should not be ignored as this transformation rapidly unfolds. To that end, we are going to arm you with the information, data, insights, and more importantly, tools and framework to understand and answer this question in your organization through digital transformation. The examples we will use are focused on how digital technologies matched with innovative thinking and reimagined business practices are changing the world we live and work in.

To give you a better perspective, let's look across four distinct but connected arenas:

- How to move from the old world to the digital world
- What drives digital and the key barriers to success
- What the framework is for getting digital right
- How to implement digital today and get on the right path for long-term growth

Thinking about your own experiences in the context of these arenas, you should agree that this will not be an easy journey nor one with a perfectly plotted pathway to success. You will fail time and time again. Failing should be something you constructively strive for, enable, and rejoice in. There are too many choices and alternatives to be perfect every time, but each failure can lead to success if you learn from your mistakes and those of others. Additionally, there are some basic principles from the old world that we should embrace on this journey to reduce some of the missteps. What is the first place where your organization is using an old view of the world to try to define your new digital DNA landscape?

PART 2

HOW DIGITAL THINKING CHANGES YOUR ACTIONS AND RESULTS

CHAPTER 3

SEVEN DRIVERS THAT WILL HELP YOU ESCAPE THE OLD WORLD

> *"Escape Velocity is about freeing your company's future from the pull of the past, but we should ask ourselves right from the start, why should one believe it is in need of liberation? What's the matter with the status quo? Why isn't 'steady as she goes' the mantra of choice, or perhaps 'stay the course'? What change is so dramatic that it calls into question the working assumptions that have sustained successful business performance for [the] past half century?"*
> —Geoffrey Moore, Escape Velocity

Almost all research on digital transformation and our own experiences with clients point to the fact that there are Seven Drivers that organizations need to understand to be successful and win in the long run. If you tap into the Seven Drivers properly, each of them (individually or as groups) will help drive much of your success in digital transformation. One of the major challenges to success with digital transformation is a lack of awareness of the forces within and around your organization. Remember the analogy of the sailing ships versus steamships we discussed earlier? Looking through the wrong lens and not recognizing the drivers can be a costly mistake.

"The difficulty lies not so much in developing new ideas as in escaping from old ones."[1]

—**John Maynard Keynes, economist**

Peter Drucker described the factors that defined moments of remarkable innovation and change in his book *Innovation and Entrepreneurship*. We see these factors more as pressures than drivers. When there is acute awareness of these pressures, often organizations can turn them into drivers for success. Digital transformations enable you to take advantage of these market tensions, which historically many organizations have tried to shield themselves from because they were not agile enough to take advantage of them. In examining Drucker's pressures, you can see many of these seven pressures are present today.

Digital Transformation Perspectives

Drucker's seven pressures are listed below:[2]

1. The Unexpected: An unexpected success, an unexpected failure, or an unexpected outside event can be a symptom of a unique opportunity.
2. The Incongruity: A discrepancy between reality and what everyone assumes it to be, or between what is and what ought to be, can create an innovative opportunity.
3. Innovation based on process need: When a weak link is evident in a particular process, but people work around it instead of doing something about it, an opportunity is available to the person or company willing to supply the "missing link."
4. Changes in industry or market structure: The opportunity for an innovative product, service, or business approach occurs when the underlying foundation of the industry or market shifts.
5. Demographics: Changes in the population's size, age structure, composition, employment, level of education, and income can create innovative opportunities.

6. Changes in perception, mood, and meaning: Innovative opportunities can develop when a society's general assumptions, attitudes, and beliefs change.
7. New Knowledge: Advances in scientific and nonscientific knowledge can create new products and new markets.

If you are looking for a new business opportunity, monitoring these seven sources may provide you with a chnace for innovation.

These pressures play a role in our Digital Revolution, and many at the same instant, depending on your industry, market, or situation. As you look these over, we challenge you to think about your own organization and ask yourself these three questions:

- Do we acknowledge these pressures in the normal course of business as we make decisions related to partners, customers, employees, and our future?
- How often does somebody raise one of these pressures as a consideration or objection when making a decision?
- Are people focusing on learning and helping others understand these pressures?

The Seven Drivers of Digital Opportunity

Although Drucker's pressures are still relevant today, the digital era has impacted and skewed them in ways he did not foresee many years ago. As such, we are seeing a new set of drivers that are specific to digital transformation. The Seven Drivers of Digital Opportunity are the key elements within the conversations that we need to focus on to thrive with digital transformation.

> "Every business should jump at the opportunity to improve and transform, especially when there are great rewards to reap, and when not doing so could be harmful. The never-ending

advancement of technology presents enterprises with countless promising opportunities for every aspect of their business."[3]

—Sven Denecken, global vice president of Strategy, Cloud Solutions, SAP

As we discuss the drivers of digital opportunity in detail, think about each through a digital-first lens. The Seven Drivers (see figure 3.1) should be a part of every conversation you have when making decisions and building strategy with peers, colleagues, and partners. Without awareness and conscious conversations about these drivers, how can you expect to have a structured approach to benefiting from a win in the digital era?

Seven Drivers of Digital Opportunity

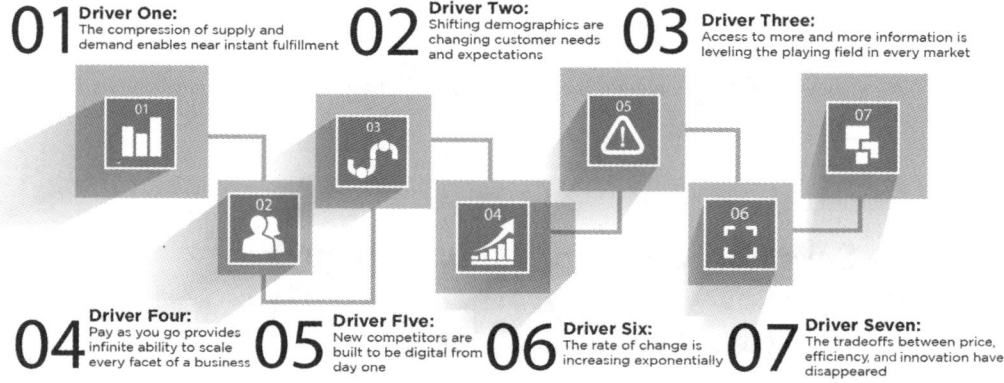

Figure 3.1: Seven Drivers of Digital Opportunity

Driver 1: The compression of supply and demand enables near instant fulfillment

Adam Smith, the father of supply and demand theory, and Paul Samuelson, the Nobel Prize–winning economist and Keynesian simplifier, would have shuddered at the immense compression taking place today between supply factors and demand elements. Historically, many businesses profited from the time lags between supply and demand by exploiting geography, knowledge, and trading practices.

Whether it is StubHub, eBay, Amazon, or any other supply-and-demand-based market, the timelines between the two have shrunk. Now the only barriers to price have become brand value, experience, and pure feature differences. Just look at Amazon. Even the oddest products have more than five hundred comments, with dozens of suppliers and differing price points. Amazon and others are working to deliver their products within the same day or hours of when a customer places an order. Near-instant gratification is almost a universal phenomenon across the Web, with instant compression occurring across everything from how we hire and find service people to how we donate money.

No longer can brands easily defend markets based on geographic control. Consider how much easier it is to make brand decisions than ever before. You can switch brands, delivery dates, and prices, and change products or suppliers with one or two clicks. Choices are delivered in targeted ways, and they are changing our tolerance for gaps in supply and demand. Where we may have tolerated certain aspects five years ago, supply and delivery options are changing even more with 3D printing, customization, and personalization happening in almost every market.

If you're still not convinced, consider these facts:

- Poor service experience led 78 percent of consumers to abandon a transaction or not make the intended purchase.[4] Can you imagine that much abandonment in a physical store?
- Apple flies many of its products in on jets from China to compress supply-and-demand time frames to hours, not days or weeks. How are other brands going to counter or keep up if they don't have Apple's margins?
- Amazon is experimenting with same-day delivery and looking at using drones and even mass transit to bypass traditional shippers and reduce delays. What could the impact be for other retail businesses and delivery services?

- Nordstrom uses in-store tablets to help customers shop across stores for delivery. As new technology is taking hold in a number of retail outlets, how will stores evolve as delivery time is also being shortened?
- Nike and Adidas allow you to create custom shoes, and many NFL teams are now creating custom 3D-printed shoes for their athletes for each game. With customizable shoes already a reality, how long will it be before you can design, order, and wear your new shoes in the same week or even in less than twenty-four hours?

Driver 2: Shifting demographics are changing customer needs and expectations

Changing demographics have significant underlying implications because we can no longer put people into nice, simple brackets. Interestingly enough, we have seen a significant compression between the generations in many ways. AARP generations surprisingly have a lot of the same characteristics as many of the other generations. Like millennials and Gen X, many of these people are online, actively working and playing in a digital world. We are using digital as a primary lens for our work and personal worlds as we get, find, and use information. Look at the decline of direct mail, event-based marketing, or traditional print-based communications. Even large and critical purchases can have little to no human contact. For example, Amazon Web Services is nearly 95 percent self-managed and hosts a large Web and cloud presence for many leading brands. We can buy cars on eBay, get house loans on Quicken, and even buy buildings online.

The debate about how each generation functions adds some spice to this conversation. Although people born after 1995 who are used to constant Internet access differ from other generations in some ways, we are increasingly seeing similarities between age groups. The act of buying life or health insurance or even a car for a baby boomer or millennial is similar because of the technologies we use every day. Regarding customization, many brands are trying to skip this debate. Think about it this way: If we build our businesses to meet the digital needs first, then provide personalization and customization to that, how much does the generation matter beyond the options provided?

Want more proof?

- 25 percent of the US population is in the millennial generation, and by 2025 they will make up 75 percent of the global workforce.[5]
- More than 70 percent of millennials expect to be self-employed at some point. Employers can no longer hope to keep employees for five to ten years, let alone for life.[6]
- 24 percent of all new American businesses in 2013 were started by people in the fifty-five to sixty-four age group, according to data from the Kauffman Firm Survey. This generation isn't retiring as soon as others and will continue to drive entrepreneurial energy and the use of the digital landscape to a large degree.[7]
- 39 percent of people now deposit checks via their mobile phones. Imagine how this weakens the intimacy and engagement with their banks.[8]

> "People—of all ages and in many markets—are constructing their own identities more freely than ever. As a result, consumption patterns are no longer defined by 'traditional' demographic segments such as age, gender, location, income, family status, and more."[9]
>
> **—Paul Backman, chief client officer, TrendWatching**

Driver 3: Access to more and more information is leveling the playing field in every market

Almost anything and everything (including national secrets, thanks to WikiLeaks and Edward Snowden) is available online, and the amount and depth of information is growing exponentially every year. From a day-to-day standpoint, secrets in pricing, customer feedback, competitive commentary, and even employees' views on working at their company (e.g., Glassdoor) are omnipresent on the Web. This means living in a digital world no longer enables information discrepancies and has fundamentally changed the way we buy, sell, interact, choose, and live. It is impossible to escape these simple realities, but time and time again we see companies and leaders ignoring the significance of how information levels the playing field and impacts how to think and act for truly successful digital transformations.

Just look at the following examples:

- William Gibson said, "The future is here; it's just not evenly distributed yet."[10] However, news of bad customer service reaches twice as many ears as praise for good service.[11] Negative information has a head start in the Digital Age.
- For every customer who complains, twenty-six remain silent.[12] Can a brand afford to have bad products when near-instant feedback is available for the asking?
- Americans tell an average of nine people about good experiences and sixteen about bad ones.[13] Does your digital strategy work to prevent this from happening or help cause it?
- In 2010, 24 percent of Americans posted comments and reviews online about the product or services they bought.[14] Soon, almost everything in B2C and B2B will be reviewed. Is your brand ready to act and respond?
- Interbrand's list of the "100 Best Global Brands" noted that eleven of the top twelve brands are currently running various types of crowdsourcing projects.[15] This statistic provides more proof that customers are in control and that design is being outsourced to the masses via digital.

"Our industry does not respect tradition—it only respects innovation. Customers are more influential than ever before. They expect speed and personalization. And they have options— lots of options. Digital technology is leveling the playing field for businesses of all sizes to disrupt their industries. It's creating opportunities to develop products and services that were once inconceivable. Size, which was once a competitive advantage, is becoming a liability as businesses that once dominated the market are now struggling to keep up with young, nimble startups. The rise of digital is going to completely disrupt businesses and dramatically change the competitive landscape. Today's leaders know that to thrive, they must transform into a digital business."[16]

—Satya Nadella, CEO, Microsoft

Driver 4: Pay-as-you-go provides infinite ability to scale every facet of a business

Due to the efficiencies digital provides, it is now commonplace to have companies with billions of dollars of revenue and a tiny number of employees. New digital businesses and business models are popping up to take advantage of the opportunities to start and run a business built on a largely digital backbone. Although this shift is not entirely new (Web 1.0 offered a glimpse of this phenomenon), the difference now is the ability to build a complete and functioning business out of virtual elements within hours. Everything from design to delivery, sales, marketing, service, and even returns are truly a few clicks away. Even CIOs in the largest Fortune organizations are increasingly adopting this "as-you-go" model. In mid-2014, Gartner talked about 70 percent of CIOs changing their sourcing models in less than three years.[17]

> "How can I get innovative, be more creative, and tap into the best minds in the industry to help me transform? That's what digital enables and what is so powerful about crowdsourcing that it enables. It's the future of work. Any business can get access to the most innovative talent in the world at a fractional rate to help a company transform. The only question is: Is your organization ready, and will you be able to handle the changes they will bring?"
>
> **—Chris Barbin, CEO, Appirio**

Consider these facts:

- Crowdsourced capital is real, but so is microfinancing across the globe. Look at the recent sensation, Flow Hive, and how it raised $2.18 million in twenty-four hours versus a $70,000 objective.[18] Who would imagine the opening up of one of the oldest pre-medieval industries in the twenty-first century?
- Goldcorp released previously secret geological data and offered $500,000 to individuals who helped the company find six million ounces of gold. The challenge yielded $3 billion in new gold in one year,[19] once again showing the power of digital to provide immense and immediate scale.
- People services such as 99Designs for graphics and Appirio/Topcoder for technical and IT skills allow you to virtualize whole departments. With a service for almost any business function, scale is achievable with just a few clicks.

"How do you build that value? Don't compromise it, but be driven by what the customer needs are. Our customers had a range of spending needs, and we wanted to gain scale and relevance around the world . . . the reality is you need to work with partners, you need to expand, and what you can't do is shrink to greatness. You've got to grow, and you've got to use your brand to grow; but you've got to treasure that brand because that's your moat around your castle."[20]

—**Ken Chenault, CEO, American Express**

Driver 5: New competitors are built to be digital from day one

Think about the up-and-comers during the past decade that have either created new business models or stolen share from established players. Tesla, for example, has shown a remarkable ability to build a revolutionary digital infrastructure for selling cars and batteries directly. First, most are built from the ground up to be digital. This provides advantages in how they listen, act, deliver, and engage. Think about it this way: Most new digital businesses recognize that customers get ideas, content, and brand value from almost infinite sources. Also, their livelihood is reliant on having information at their fingertips to drive fast, empowered decisions and plan just enough ahead to be competitive but not overly committed to one narrow or singular strategy. Also, even the most advanced marketing, social, and listening tools are purchased by the seat or user. This gives startups the same power to understand, engage, and look for opportunities in marketing that traditional brands have and use daily.

The challenge is discovering how to build these capabilities into huge organizations. Many are trying, and Zappos may be the most revolutionary example. The company has experimented with shifting its entire organizational structure so that almost all of its 1,500 employees no longer work for a manager. Rather than being accountable to a single boss in a traditional hierarchy, each employee reports to the other people in their circles. Then each circle is tasked with an organizational goal to achieve, and each role that people fill within the circle is a task necessary for accomplishing that goal. Ultimately, this management structure, called "Holacracy," is being morphed from its original vision as they tweak and refine the process and system to design a new organizational structure to handle the challenges they have experienced and keep them on the front of the wave.

And these trends are continuing: Business Insider argues that only $750,000 to $1.5 million is needed to take a new product to market or a startup.[21] This is but a fraction of what most large organizations spend.

Crowdfunding is changing the way individuals and organizations raise money. GoFundMe has raised more than $3 billion for personal fund-raisers. Kickstarter raised $444 million in 2014 alone.[22] Digital has removed the funding barrier that stymied many startups in the past. About 18 percent of entrepreneurs succeed in their first venture.[23] This again shows how the digital tools available to startups are making a growing number successful right out of the gate. Kickstarter has launched more than ninety-eight thousand new projects and raised $521 million in its first four years of existence.[24] Crowdsourcing is now becoming mainstream as even larger brands are tapping into the power to test and fund products socially. According to Kickstarter, only 10 percent of projects that raise more than 30 percent of their goal end up failing, and only 3 percent fail that surpass 50 percent funding.[25] When the market votes, businesses tend to succeed. This provides an easy way of testing and verifying ideas faster and more cheaply than traditional launches.

Harvard University noted that 72 percent of startup founders today are just coming off previous positions as director or higher roles at other businesses.[26] This means they have the knowledge to build something new while tapping into virtual resources and new funding to build from the ground up.

Only 7 percent of Gen Y works for a Fortune 500 company. Startups dominate the workforce for this demographic.[27] This is a big challenge for large organizations looking to tap this market going forward.

> "Creating value with digital assets has been inherent in every leadership role at Amazon and similar digital native companies from day one, and it's a big part of their success."[28]
>
> —**Jeff Bezos, CEO, Amazon**

Driver 6: The rate of change is extremely exponential

Change is more rapid now than ever before. In the past century, the benchmark for change was about thirty years or so. Transitions from sail to steam, propeller to jet, and mainframes to PCs happened in about that timespan. Thirty years in the digital era feels like an eternity. Evolutions and even revolutions are happening within years or at most a decade. Organizations will not have time to hide from these realities. Those that digitally transform will need an infrastructure capable of listening, assessing, and appropriately adjusting to the very nature of these changes.

> "If the rate of change on the outside exceeds the rate of change on the inside, the end is near."[29]
>
> —**Jack Welch, former chairman and CEO, General Electric**

To give you some context, a decade is a mere twenty-five hundred working days. Now, businesses are privy to constant feedback that is highlighting new paths, pitfalls, and opportunities every day. It would be easy to dismiss, but think about what has happened with the Apple Watch. Rolex and Tag Heuer now have a new competitor—equal if not greater in size and market share— with more than $2 billion in sales virtually overnight.

This one launch stole—or created depending on your perspective—30 percent market share in the luxury end of the market in less than one year. This is against brands that have more than 150 years of market success. Plus, Apple is expanding the market with watch apps, accompanying services, and add-ons. Apple has shown how quickly a brand can diminish a hundred years of market importance, not to mention relegating many smartwatch makers to also-rans in terms of market share.

The rate of change is impacting us now and in the future: Half of the information taught to first-year science undergraduates will be obsolete by the time they graduate,[30] and 65 percent of children who are now in preschool will work in jobs that do not exist today.[31] Nothing else exemplifies the pace of change and shows the need to keep up like these statistics.

More than 40 percent of the companies that were at the top of the Fortune 500 list in 2000 were no longer there in 2010.[32] The roles of businesses are now being rewritten at a faster pace than ever before.

The price of storing a bit of information has dropped 60 percent a year for six decades.[33] Combined with the insights provided by big data and technology becoming more mobile, we will soon live in a world where almost everything is recorded, stored, and analyzed in near real time.

About 73 percent of people surveyed said they wouldn't care if the brands they use disappeared from their lives.[34] Consumers are getting used to the pace of change and are far more comfortable with new providers coming in to meet their changing needs.

There are now more mobile connected devices than people on earth.[35] Everyone can see that the mobile shift is significant. But how does the world look, and how do brands respond and function when we are mobile all the time?

Crowd thinking has replaced most forms of peer research. If you examine the challenge that political polling now has, you can see that there is no such thing as a random sample of a population. How you manage to filter out the noise from signals as well as embrace the full nature of crowd thinking is a vital component for success. How are businesses going to separate the good from the clutter when leveraging the public for primary research?

Digital Transformation Tools

The question becomes: How do existing brands deal with the pressure of constant and exponential change? In the past, large signals and clear signs preceded major shifts. The new model is much more about seeing faint signals and understanding how they are evolving from even nascent quarters of the ecosystem. Figure 3.2 is designed to help brands identify and think about the constant change in the Digital Age.

Trend Spotting & Tracking Template

It is very easy to pay attention to what ultimately is noise in the digital age. The vast array of content flowing freely means it is now more important to focus on filtering than gathering.
The very best companies use a model similar to this in order to help filter noise for threats and opportunities. The key is to identify value in the information you see. Using the columns in this chart will help you identify a blip or a trend with velocity before it becomes mainstream. It will also help you predict what that information looks like and where it comes from. This is not pure science, but given the very rapid nature of change and the immense range of sources that allows you to very quickly build the right frameworks for rapid and ongoing decisions. Imagine you were a brand manager at Swatch a number of years ago and you first saw smart watches as an idea. If you would have used this type of architecture you could have far better predicted the rise of this category and better monitored and plotted your course.

	Visible Connections & Blips — **VISIBLE**	Trend with Velocity — **VELOCITY**	Vindicated to Mainstream — **VINDICATED**
Definition	Pockets of blips that are at best 5% connected to the mainstream behaviors.	Connected to core behaviors for a number of key segments.	Moving to mainstream behavior for core market, no longer a trend.
Early Signs			
False Indicators			
Cross Over Signs To Next Stage			
Getting Internal Attention			
External Measure			

Figure 3.2: Trend Spotting and Tracking Template

Brand marketers, communications professionals, and sales and product development people should print out this chart and use it as a daily reminder of how to think about change and digital opportunities. To use it, take the information you are hearing, seeing, and dealing with every day and drop it into one of these cells. Imagine you are a brand manager at Rolex and you are thinking about the luxury end of the watch market two years ago, one year ago, and now. Imagine if you had used this matrix two years ago to think about the potential for luxury wearables with early indicators from social conversations or internal water cooler chat. We have to wonder how much better watchmakers could have responded if they had been looking at wide sets of data. What is they'd taken advantage of insight ripples rather than just looking for the traditional huge one-off market signal?

Driver 7: The trade-offs between price, efficiency, and innovation have disappeared

Clayton Christensen's important theory in *The Innovator's Dilemma*[36] laid out key types of innovation, including pioneering innovation, innovation in best practices, and technological innovations. Basically the theory states that businesses have three clear paths to success: cut prices, be more efficient, or invest in sustained technological advantages. Digital enables you to do all three simultaneously. To give you an example, look at American Airlines. The company moved to iPads for its pilots in 2013, saving more than $1.2 million a year in associated fuel costs by eliminating the need for the hefty logs and files as well as the large briefcases used to carry them. Right after American Airlines' move, Southwest Airlines, the traditional low-fare leader, announced it was changing its decades-old reservation system to be more efficient and provide far more automation. Executives at Southwest have branded it "Transfarency," because they have accepted the inevitable compression of knowledge between their crowds and themselves.

Just fifteen months apart, two stalwart airlines moved to be more digital, lowered costs, and increased their effectiveness to be more competitive.

"From a digital perspective, our big banner is go where the customers are. Our job is to make sure that not only does the information present itself clearly and crisply for both the customers and our internal teams, but the information most needed is intuitive and easy to use. Everything is more converged today than it's ever been. With this information, listening to the customer relentlessly and the openness to test and learn, we as a company have the freedom to take intelligent risks. Any innovation that can come from a customer suggestion or a front-line employee could turn into something big."
—**Linda Rutherford, vice president and chief communications officer, Southwest Airlines**

If we look at crowdsourcing ideas from internal resources, we can see how the shift in these Seven Drivers includes plenty of opportunity for those organizations wishing to grasp the shift in demographics, attitudes, or compression of supply and demand. A Cap Gemini and MIT joint study titled "The Digital Advantage: How Digital Leaders Outperform Their Peers in Every Industry" also eloquently argues that the economic outputs of digital leadership can be seen in revenue growth, profitability, and market valuation.[37] All produced immensely positive outcomes, including—

- More than 9 percent for revenue generation for the leading segment over others
- More than 26 percent differences in profitability
- 12 percent increase in market valuations

Figure 3.3 explains Cap Gemini and MIT's views on the myths and realities of digital transformation.

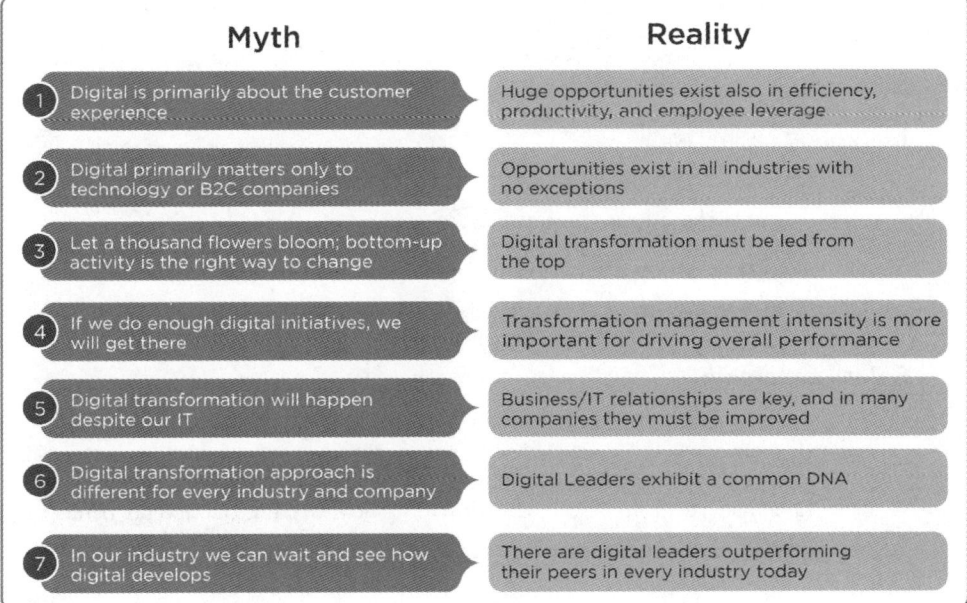

Figure 3.3: Digital Transformation Reality Check[38]

What's the Bottom Line?

Few organizations are experiencing all these pressures equally at one time, or even in the same sequence. To help organizations identify the key elements affecting them, we have included a quick audit to share among your colleagues. As you move through the following questions, remember to consider the consequences so your transformation efforts will allow you to thrive.

Think about these questions in each of the current roles you have in the organization, and see whether you are adequately paying attention to the pressures that are sculpting the world around you. First take the audit yourself. Then sit with a colleague or work team and assess the level of attention and action you are taking against each of the Seven Drivers.

Executive Leadership
- Are you thinking about promoting or hiring people based on their understanding of these drivers and the upsides they offer you?

- Have you decided which of these drivers offer you the best strategic advantage or present the biggest risk moving forward?

Marketing Leadership
- How much time are you asking your senior leaders to spend talking and thinking about these drivers?
- Are you thinking about technologies and insights that will help take advantage of any of these drivers?

Sales Leadership
- Is your sales team feeding data back to you on any of these Seven Drivers?
- Have you thought about the skills and knowledge needed in three years to take advantage of these drivers?

Product Development
- In your planning process, are any of these Seven Drivers part of the debate?
- Have you ever thought about which one of these drivers could affect the shape and nature of the products and services you have traditionally delivered?

Human Capital Leadership
- Do you recruit with a perspective on any of these Seven Drivers?
- During interviews, are potential employees talking about any of these drivers and their potential skills to help take advantage of them?

Technology Leadership
- How important are these drivers in influencing the technology recommendations you make?
- Are you open to throwing away technologies based on any of these Seven Drivers?

The Future Is Digital and the Winners Are Being Built Now

Almost universally, executives clearly understand the need to be more digital. However, it is not easy for many to know when, where, or how to move toward digital and away from the old ways of business that will hold them back. The trick is to move smartly and to navigate the right digital course for each group or line of business within the organization. This is not about recklessly abandoning what you already have or experimenting with small tests across the organization. Rather, it is much more about constructing a strategy to identify how to bring elements within the organization together to gain significant benefits and reap even more benefits with each addition. In many occasions, the best combination will come from the old with new skills, technologies, processes, and mindsets applied or added.

If all of this sounds logical and straightforward, you are not alone. But if the drivers are so obvious, why aren't more of us achieving breakthrough results?

Digital Transformation Tools

As a companion to the questionnaire, we've included an organizational audit, figure 3.4, to help identify the key drivers and their overall impact to your business.

Seven Drivers of Digital Opportunity

Using the scale below, score your organization.

1. We do not collectively believe this is a pressure or opportunity for us.
2. Groups talk about acting on this but are not in active development yet.
3. We have been changing some small elements of our business to respond to this.
4. We have seen the results of experiments that imply what the upside could be for us with this pressure.
5. We are formulating more extensive plans around this pressure and looking to make changes in how we think and enable other parts of the organization too.
6. Key parts of our business are now paying attention to how they perform based on this pressure.
7. We will be fully embracing this pressure in our next strategic business planning cycle. That means appropriate resources and new ways to do business.
8. We have fully embraced this pressure over two years ago and it now is a key asset for us in how we talk about the company or organization.
9. Our business is increasingly focused on this pressure as an advantage for us having seen plenty of results.
10. Our business is extremely focused on this pressure as an advantage for us having seen plenty of results.

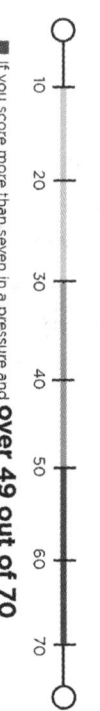

- If you score more than seven in a pressure and **over 49 out of 70** in total, then you should be on the voyage to a significant digital transformation.
- If you score **between 30 and 49**, then some pressures are likely dominating your mindset and having full experiments or key ecosystems leading the charge will be key for future success.
- If you score **lower than 30**, we would recommend you take a hard look at the nature of your industry or segment because other organizations in your competitive set are taking a more aggressive pathway to digital transformation.

Figure 3.4: The Seven Drivers of Digital Opportunity

Driver One:
The compression of supply and demand from what we experienced three to five years ago

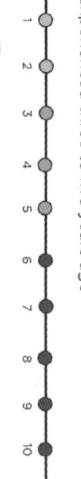

Driver Two:
A shift in demographics in our customer base and/or a different sense of customer entitlement

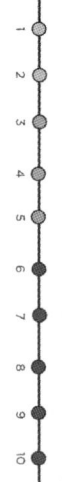

Driver Three:
Customers, partners, competitors, and employees have more information than ever before

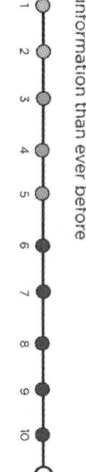

Driver Four:
The idea of the near immediate ability to get scale at the drop of a hat

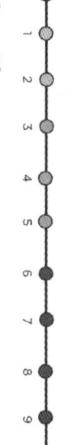

Driver Five:
Start-ups in our segment or industry present a threat

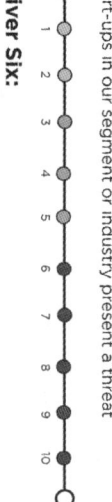

Driver Six:
Change is a constant

Driver Seven:
The paradox of lower costs and efficiency with real innovation

CHAPTER 4

THE TAO OF GETTING DIGITAL DONE RIGHT AND OVERCOMING OURSELVES

> *"The competitor to be feared is one who never bothers about you at all, but goes on making his own business better all the time."*
> —Henry Ford

As we mentioned, the need for digital transformation should feel obvious and logical. We experience it both personally and professionally in some way, every day. Yet digital transformation is still a major struggle for organizations. Even the ones that are succeeding will tell you they have failed just as many times as they have succeeded. Why can something so sensible and apparent be so hard to get right? The simple answer is that ample evidence suggests that strong undercurrents linked to challenges and old-world thinking are preventing our success. In addition, there are fallacious assumptions about what it takes to overcome them and thrive with digital transformation, today and in the future.

> "Quantum theory thus reveals a basic oneness of the universe. It shows that we cannot decompose the world into independently existing smallest units. As we penetrate into matter, nature does not show us any isolated 'building blocks,' but rather appears as

a complicated web of relations between the various parts of the whole. These relations always include the observer in an essential way. The human observer constitutes the final link in the chain of observational processes, and the properties of any atomic object can be understood only in terms of the object's interaction with the observer."[1]

—**Fritjof Capra, author of** *Tao of Physics: An Exploration of the Parallels Between Modern Physics and Eastern Mysticism*

Organizations need to understand the challenges to success, see how these challenges interact within the organization to prevent success, and get real, practical advice on how to avoid these obstacles. From our extensive research and client experience, we have identified seven core challenges that act together to prevent success with digital transformation. Understanding these and maneuvering away from and around them is the key to building a successful digital organization.

Figure 4.1 provides a quick overview of the Seven Challenges. A more detailed deep dive with ideas about how to identify and avoid these challenges in your organization will be discussed in chapter 5.

1. Executive Mandates Are Not Enough

The complexity that lies within successful digital transformations cannot be underestimated. Simply declaring intent is more dangerous than helpful because doing so drastically underestimates what it takes to get digital transformation right. Evidence shows us that executive engagement is vital across all activities. According to our research with PulsePoint Group and the Economist Intelligence Unit, the most successful brands incorporated the active engagement of the CEO or executive leader in five areas (governance, content delivery, resource allocations, metrics development, and active advocacy) across the organization. Brands failing to digitally transform had the executive engaged in just one thing—mandating action (like having the executive use social media themselves).

Figure 4.1: The Seven Challenges to Doing Digital Right

2. Expectations Chasm

Commitment to digital transformation may be well meaning, but the failure to deliver real economic value often leads to mass withdrawal from the process within and across the organization. Two years of tracking research shows us that withdrawal is inevitable if expectations severely exceed the reality of what you can actually build and deliver. From wave one to wave two of our social digital transformation research, we saw major segments retreat in their commitment because of failures. Essentially, 24 percent of all Fortune organizations retreated from midlevel commitments to digital transformation to the lowest possible commitment levels.

3. Digital Requires Both a Village and Architecture

In many cases, executives have found it best to move fast in launching new initiatives to avoid organizational inertia and hurdles that prevent or delay action. In digital transformation, we have found a significant contradiction that shows speed comes from the combination of two elements:

a. Architecting the right larger framework (with metrics and enablement such as training and systems to get near-instant scale)
b. Building a wide range and degree of advocacy for digital projects within the organization

In fact, the most successful social digital transformations are based on indexing across one hundred key variables including mostly long-term architecture and process- and enablement-based activities. The end result is businesses that build this level of architecture can act on information and market changes twice as fast and often more successfully overall than organizations that act fast with little architecture and process. The research showed that these successful organizations went from 145 days to design, execute, and measure a new program to just 74 days. Also, failed social digital transformations tend to have only one to three departments or functions engaged, while the most successful social digital transformations involve the active engagement of eleven distinctive departments or functions.

4. Digital Takes Different Metrics

In a digital world, measurement becomes the thermometer for success. In most cases, organizations skew toward the simple measure of volume to gauge efforts. But the data from successful organizations shows the best measurements are a synthesis of four types of metrics: volume-based metrics, engagement, advocacy, and abandonment. Note that small amounts of abandonment like a shopping basket or a social feed can be a key indicator of near-future challenges. Smart brands focus much more on these key indicator metrics than only on volume-focused metrics. Also, 25 percent of the metrics used by winning brands in social/digital transformation focus on softer perceptual metrics.

5. Success Comes from the Inside Out, Not from Outside In

When the impetus to be more digital hits an organization, the tendency of most leaders is to make it happen fast by outsourcing suppliers to take over key parts of delivery and process building. However, a successful digital transformation requires that the core competency resides inside the organization. The most successful organizations build the right skills and resources needed for digital internally. As we discussed in challenge 3, transformation takes a village and an architecture. The most successful brands own 85 percent of the production for social digital transformation across four types of execution groups and only outsource 15 percent of the efforts.

6. Openness to Alternative Strategies Drives Digital

Most organizations become successful by developing a clear strategy, agreeing on a sequence of tactical activities, and tracking metrics to measure efforts. While these strategies are still required, leading performers in digital transformation aggressively pursue alternative options via numerous experiments before locking down a course. This small but significant adjustment enables leaders to leverage the insights digital provides in a fast and efficient manner without derailing the entire organization or constantly re-strategizing. Two of the key elements to success are the ability to drive extensive experimentation and to perform a full review of alternative strategies before executing digital transformation activities. Only the best economic performers do both. In addition, of all the types of engagement platforms and social content, the best economic performers leverage just eleven platforms and four types of content. Overall, these leaders achieve stellar results by focusing on only 44 of the 1,530 possible scenarios, or just 2.8 percent of the total combinations of platforms and content.

7. Digital Is Not Just Customer Focused

While many organizations started with or have seen the most success with digital transformation in customer-focused arenas, the best performers leverage digital to drive greater value across the business. Expanding smartly to tie efforts across the organization is a key ingredient that delivers on what your customers want. The most successful social digital transformations involve at least twelve different ways of using transformation to drive change in customer service, employees, crowdsourcing ideas, demand, communications, internal collaboration, etc. Most organizations that failed focused on fewer than four ways.

Most Feel the Effects of the Challenges

No matter where you look, there is almost a universal level of clarity of these or similar challenges. Research from Altimeter, Deloitte, McKinsey, and many consultants all argue for the same points:

- Executive leadership needs to get on the bandwagon.
- Teams need to be corralled and engaged.
- Customers need increasing focus.
- Cross-functional teams need to be set up.
- IT leadership needs to be part of the process and the solution.

"Developing a culture that brings out the very best in people is such a significant part of success because the need to evolve and respond quickly is a key part of what makes high-performing organizations and teams uniquely qualified in our digital world. In sport or in business or government. Only humans have that innate ability but it needs to be brought out.

"A leader or a coach's role is to elevate people's performance and try to help them be their best. To make this work, we [the Seattle Seahawks] have established a relationship-based approach that helps all leaders understand the individuals that we work with and analyze and figure them out, to make sense of what's important to them and how they operate. Through kind of a relationship and ongoing two-way communication any team member can be directed with the purpose of helping them consistently find their best. This starts by creating an environment where they feel comfortable and feel that they are accepted and feel that they have their best chance to be heard as well as to learn. Millennials are inherently interested in being the very best versions of themselves because they recognize that this is maybe the only thing they have control over in a constantly evolving digital world."
—**Pete Carroll, head coach, Super Bowl Champion Seattle Seahawks**

None of these points are wrong, but it is not any more useful than telling you hard work will make you rich and successful. If this was all you needed, the world would be run by single parents with two jobs, who arguably work harder and longer than anyone. To get past the challenges, you need to understand how each of these points impacts your digital transformation (both at an individual and organizational level) as well as have the strategies to move forward that create a set of components that work in one smooth system. In fact, the last three years of research on digital transformation and social media with more than a thousand case studies and more than fifteen hundred interviews with executives shows that, much like the world of physics and biology, there are unique indicators for success that go far beyond the typical view of semi-independent components.

> "There is no silver bullet—and while some factors have more impact than others on a transformation's outcome, the real magic happens when these actions are pursued together."[2]
> —David Jacquemont, Dana Maor, and Angelika Reich

The secret to overcoming these Seven Challenges is to see them within the confines of failed digital transformation processes. Failures invariably teach us far more than success. This is in part because failure is much more common, and the rationale behind success can be difficult to explain and illustrate in simple terms.

> "I have not failed. I've just found ten thousand ways that won't work."
> —Thomas. A. Edison

If We Truly Understand the Nature of Failure, We Get a Head Start on Understanding Success

As with Edison, many organizations are finding a large number of ways digital transformation does not work. Understanding and avoiding the Seven Challenges will greatly improve your odds of finding a way digital transformation *will* work. How are we so sure? Extensive cause-and-effect analysis across more than fifteen types of engagement including crowdsourcing, demand generation, employee management, executive communications, work collaboration, and interviews with CEOs, CFOs, CIOs, CMOs, and specialists point the way and highlight the issues. Combine these findings with economic performance indicators and we see clear empirical evidence for why failure occurs across a whole range of interconnected elements:

- Preparedness factors
- Investment mindsets
- Strategic models and frameworks

- Sequencing of activities and resources
- Collaboration factors
- Measurement models
- Timelines for success
- Economic metrics
- Executional focus (media and content)
- Levels and range of advocacy

Looking at this data, we also see the Seven Challenges most of these elements fall into. While not everything fits into the seven, we estimate that these are the largest and more significant items that derail digital transformation projects. Further, many of these failures that don't fit neatly tend to be the result of the Seven Challenges to digital transformation and not part of the root cause.

Digital Transformation Perspective

The segmentation model, figure 4.2, is from PulsePoint Group's Social Media Accelerator research. This is a wonderful proxy for the whole digital transformation because it is focused on a rich vein of business-defined digital activities designed to solve digital-age challenges such as idea generation, employee collaboration, customer intimacy, and cocreation opportunities. Each segment was produced using an analysis that grouped performance for the key underlying factors mentioned above. This allowed us to see the inner DNA of winners, those struggling, and those organizations really standing on the edge. Almost a thousand interviews and more than 2,700 tested scenarios provided us with a deep pool of understanding about what lies behind success and failure. We named the segments based on some simple ideas:

- **Trailblazers:** They do one form of social transformation really well (often customer service and support), but they seem to have little intent or architecture in place to do anything else or move beyond their initial efforts.

- Observers: They have barely put their feet in the water and have lost or never really built an extensive strategy or process.
- Creators: They have a number of social transformation projects and activities in place, but each yields different results, and support, measurement, and enablement are patchy. Creators have become successful in pockets but not across every area.
- Incrementalists: Like Creators, Incrementalists transform socially but struggle to get measured returns and have stalled in their desire to do more.
- Thrivers: They are the leaders across the key components. Thrivers create buy-in and enable processes across their organizations with exceptional measurement architectures. They do not overexecute or rely enough on external partners to get real scale and buy-in.
- Dreamers: Dreamers undertake many of the actions that the Thrivers do, but the big chasm here is the failure to have a measurement system in place.

As you can see in the segmentation model (figure 4.2), the return for each group varied depending on the group and level of commitment. It is interesting to note the change from wave one of our research in 2012 to wave two in 2013.

"Individually, we are one drop. Together, we are an ocean."
—**Ryunosuke Satoro, Japanese writer**

The vast majority of the leaders we interviewed say the key to overcoming the Seven Challenges is focusing on real, practical advice on how to avoid them in the first place. Now that you have seen an overview of the challenges to success, we need to dive deeper to see how they interact to prevent success across the organization. Which of the Seven Challenges represents the biggest hurdles for your organization, now and in the future? Does your answer change if you think about the seven across different departments or implementations?

Digital Transformation Perspective

The segmentation model below is from PulsePoint Groups Social Media Accelerator. As we stated before, this is a wonderful proxy for the whole digital transformation because it is focused on a rich vein of business-defined digital activities designed to solve digital-age challenges such as idea generation, employee collaboration, and customer intimacy and cocreation opportunities. Each segment was produced using an analysis that grouped performance for all the key underlying factors mentioned previously. This way we get to see the inner DNA of winners, those struggling, and those organizations really standing on the edge. Some 1,000 interviews and over 2,700 tested scenarios give us a very deep pool of understanding about what sits behind success and failure. We named the segments based on some simple ideas.

Trailblazers
They do one form of social transformation really well, often customer service and support, but seem to have little intent or architecture in place to do anything else or next.

Incrementalists
Like Creators, they do a number of forms of social transformation but mightily struggle to get measured returns and have stalled in their desire to do more.

Thrivers
They are the leaders, with all the key components buy-in, and enabling processes in place with exceptional measurement architectures.

Observers
They barely put their feet in the water and have lost or never really built an extensive strategy process.

Creators
They have a number of social transformation projects and activities in place but each yields different results and support, measurement, and enablement are patchy. They have become successful in pockets but not across every area.

Dreamers
They perform many of the actions that the Thrivers do, but the big chasm here is the failure to have a measurement system in place.

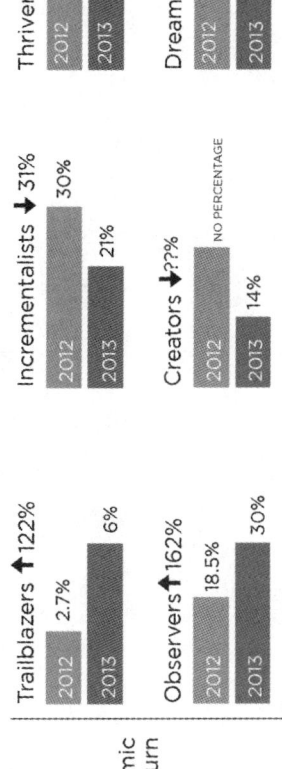

Figure 4.2: Learning the Pathway to Digital Transformation from Social Engagement

CHAPTER 5

DIVING DEEP INTO THE SEVEN CHALLENGES TO DIGITAL TRANSFORMATION

"Twenty years from now you will be more disappointed by the things that you didn't do than by the ones you did do, so throw off the bowlines, sail away from safe harbor, catch the trade winds in your sails. Explore. Dream. Discover."
—Mark Twain

The overview in chapter 4 should have provided you with a quick and easy way to understand the Seven Challenges. The hard part is systematically identifying which of the seven are either preventing successes today or have the potential to derail your organization's transformation progress.

"Digital Darwinism is a fate that threatens most organizations in almost every industry. Because of this, businesses not only have to compete for today but also for the foreseeable future. Digital Darwinism is the phenomenon when technology and society evolve faster than an organization can adapt. There are many reasons for this of course. Every fabric of a company is strained due to internal and external influences. The challenge lies among the very leaders running the show today. Their mission and

Seven Challenges To Doing Digital Right

How does your organization score?
1 = strongly disagree; 10 = strongly agree

Figure 5.1: The Seven Challenges to Doing Digital Right

the processes and systems they support today may already be working against them."[1]

—Brian Solis, principal analyst, Altimeter Group

The research that we and numerous others have conducted shows clear evidence that these Seven Challenges (figure 5.1) are causing organizations to fail or deliver far below their potential.

Executive Mandates Are Not Enough

To fundamentally enable the process of digital transformation, leaders must go beyond mandates and encouragement by working with teams on the front lines. To move beyond the mere act of cheerleading for digital transformation, leaders must realize there are sets of parallel challenges to conquer. Organizations that took a rigorous, action-oriented approach led by executives reported a 79 percent success rate—three times the average for all transformations. In addition, senior managers who engaged and communicated openly across the organization about the progress of the transformation were eight times more likely to report a successful transformation compared to those who did not engage in open communication. This level of engagement has an even greater effect on enterprise-wide transformations, where change efforts are 12.4 times more likely to be successful.

> "Leadership through digital transformation has to come from the very top. Executives can't just say it. They have to live it. This includes understanding they can't be experts in everything, but they have to know enough to understand where they are weak. Think about it this way, the average age of a CEO is roughly fifty-five, so most did not grow up in a digital world. So they must work that much harder to live digitally. Without this extra effort, many businesses will fail at digital transformation until the next generation moves into executive positions."
>
> —Bruce Rogers, chief insights officer, *Forbes*

To succeed, executives need to overcome a number of parallel challenges. The first challenge to overcome is actions vs. encouragement. This may seem obvious, but executives need to get their hands dirty. McKinsey conducted research that determined twenty-four practical actions that organizations could take in digital transformation. The vast majority of these are communication and coordination initiatives that require executive action, not just mandates or cheerleading. Some of McKinsey's practical actions include—

- Senior managers communicated openly across the organization about the transformation's progress and success.
- Leaders modeled the behavior changes they were asking employees to make.
- Senior managers communicated openly across the organization about the transformation's implications for individuals' day-to-day work.
- The organization developed its people so that they could surpass expectations for performance.
- Performance evaluations held initiative leaders accountable for their transformation contributions.
- Leaders used a consistent change story they shared across the organization to align the organization around its transformation goals.
- Roles and responsibilities in the transformation were clearly defined.
- Sufficient personnel were allocated to support initiative implementation.
- A capability-building program was designed to enable employees to meet transformation goals.
- Leaders of initiatives received change leadership training during the transformation.

As you can see from the list above, leadership needs to make digital transformation part of the organization's fabric via reviews, resourcing, training, goal setting, and other top-down initiatives. Failure to deliver active and deep executive involvement pushes the organization down an inefficient and problematic path. Pockets in the organization form to heed the executive mandate and become more efficient. This invariably leads to clashes between departments as well as resource, goal, and strategy conflicts at an organizational level. These issues induce nearly the exact opposite of digital transformation's goal—inefficiency. With groups and teams competing against each other or working in silos instead of collaborating, executives are forced to become arbiters of the problems. The end result is the organization and its leaders are forced away from the strategy and goals of the business and pushed toward wasting time and effort by managing the tactical issues they created as a result of not being fully involved.

The second challenge is the incapacity of the leadership to get the range and process for digital transformation outside their own expressions and interest areas. If your executive leadership does not build advocate groups, widen metrics beyond volumetric measures, and set aside new (not replacement) budgets for these endeavors, then their mandates are, at worst, hollow and, at best, ill thought out.

It is great to lead from the top, but great digital leadership involves leadership across the spectrum. When we compared the highest economic performers to the lowest, we saw clear indicators for failure and success. The secret is collective buy-in, collective enablement, and a focus on using the right metrics. The organizations that outperformed their competitors used their leadership positions to fully enable the actions of their teams. The bottom line is that executives have a crucial and deep role to play in digital transformation. Providing a mandate without being involved or blindly signing checks to start digital projects without elevating efforts to organizational goals leads to significant long-term setbacks that few organizations can overcome.

Digital Transformation Perspectives

Many come to mind when we think of executives changing the fabric of an organization. Yet few have been successful and few have become digital explorers like Angela Ahrendts, then CEO of Burberry and now Apple's senior vice president of retail and online stores.

At the time Ahrendts became CEO, Burberry was significantly falling behind in the overall luxury retail sector. The sector was growing at a rate of more than 12 percent a year, yet the company only saw 2 percent growth. Ahrendts knew a change was needed to keep up with and eventually surpass the competition. Rather than just adding digital, Ahrendts and Burberry decided to use digital across the entire organization to leapfrog their competitors. During Burberry's transformation, digital was involved in every aspect of the business and became the catalyst for every change. As Ahrendts said, "When we set out to build our strategy, we said that we didn't just want to be a great brand—we wanted to be a great company to work for and to empower our young, digitally native workforce. We tell the team constantly that the bigger we get, the closer we have to work and the more connected we have to be—and technology is the key connector."

Below are a few of the digital changes Ahrendts spearheaded with her teams during Burberry's digital transformation:[2]

- Partnering with technology companies to create a retail theater, which allowed Burberry to broadcast their multifaceted content to stores globally.
- Live-streaming runway shows in stores and enabling customers to shop the collection on iPads right afterward, for delivery in six to eight weeks.
- With the help of Salesforce.com, joining its existing platforms with new communication and analytic tools. Salesforce.com's CRM modules were deployed across the entire business.
- Creating a strategic innovation council chaired by chief creative officer Christopher Bailey. It includes forward-thinking directors who are able to share ideas and dreams. Senior executives and key internal teams are then responsible for putting the dreams into action.

"In digital, we are ahead of most of our competitors because we have been on this journey for the last six years. We are beginning to blur the lines between physical stores and the digital experience. More people see the brand via digital than any other medium."[3]

—**Angela Ahrendts, former CEO, Burberry, currently senior vice president of retail and online stores, Apple**

Expectations Chasm

Throughout our research, we were able to see how less than stellar success in digital transformation projects led to mass withdrawal from the process across the organization. The number one reason for this withdrawal is that digital expectations severely exceed the reality of what is built and delivered. The key issue is the process by which digital projects are sold into the organization. No one consciously oversells the benefits of a project to get buy-in. However, racing to keep up or to get ahead, as well as the omnipresent information on the benefits of digital transformation projects, does tend to push some teams toward creating lofty expectations. This expectation chasm becomes a naysayer's paradise.

Thinking back to the issues described in the executive mandate challenge, the fight for resources as well as political standing in the organization often bring out the wolves when a project does not deliver. At that point, everyone in the business with a different opinion or priority has carte blanche to use the failure as a proof point for his or her initiative or strategy. It is no wonder that this chasm creates pullback as the business licks its wounds and attempts to do a postmortem on the failure. In some cases, results are achieved but oversold. In other instances, poor planning or execution leads to subpar outcomes. Either way, the organization's appetite for digital takes a hit, and now every new digital project has a new hurdle to overcome.

The lesson is that commitment and interest can easily be dampened by failures in a short period. With more than eight in ten executives buying into digital transformation, but less than 16 percent of organizations winning, it is statistically likely you are one of the organizations struggling. Failure to deliver or scale properly takes you off the winning path as organizations reduce intent, support, and energy. This phenomenon has occurred for years, and many of us can remember stalled CRM or other Web 1.0 projects that left technologies radically underutilized when employees didn't quite get it. But in the digital era, everything is designed to work together and build on each other. Thus, a failure to set realistic expectations in digital often leads to full retreat or reevaluation from digital transformation opportunities.

It is essential to make the right choices in the right way across every facet from design to delivery to measurement. Expectation setting in this complicated environment is difficult. Failure to lay out an extended plan and progress are key reasons many organizations are still struggling to win now with their digital transformation investments.

Digital Transformation Perspectives

When thinking about an expectations chasm, few would disagree that the launch of the healthcare.gov website and health insurance program suffered from a classic case of overpromising and underdelivering. While the healthcare.gov website did get off the ground and successfully launched, few if any nongovernmental organizations have the resources or desire to push through a program fraught with underdelivery. Any CEO or board faced with the same issues would have pulled back on this and other transformation efforts. It is important to recognize that many issues cascaded together in the healthcare.gov launch, much as they do in business. Leaders need to be aware of how issues like these creep into digital transformation projects to doom not only the project but also push the organization into digital withdrawal.

Unrealistic Requirements

With healthcare.gov the promise was easy integration in a single site of hundreds of options linked to a multitude of suppliers with secure log-ins, enrollment, and eligibility checking. This combination at this scale had never been attempted before. In business, many digital projects are announced as the simple solution to solve a corporate problem (e.g., once we have a salesforce, sales will be fixed/greatly improved), but digital is not a simple fix. Digital is a set of principles that requires many coordinated elements to drive value.

Integration Needs

For healthcare.gov, the system and architecture required to integrate its various functions and partners in order to deliver easy consumer use was greatly underestimated. In total, fifty-five contractors, five federal agencies, thirty-six states, and three hundred private sector insurers offering well over four thousand plans had to come together in one system. In business, like with healthcare.gov, many moving pieces need to be integrated, and not doing so leads to overall failure. Departments, suppliers, customers, and vendors all have to be integrated into a business's digital effort to reap the rewards promised.

Fragmented Authority

With healthcare.gov, there was a great deal of infighting between different parts of the bureaucracy contending for control—the IT shop, the policy shop, and the communications shop. Key decisions were often delayed, guidance to contractors was inconsistent, and nobody seemed truly in charge. In business, the same can be true for conflicts and power struggles that occur among departments and leaders when communication and collaboration are not part of the digital culture.

Loose Metrics

The teams leading healthcare.gov didn't initially have adequate or consistent ways of measuring progress. Absence of reliable metrics helps explain why federal officials didn't realize until late in the game that healthcare.gov might not be ready for prime time. As with business, the right metrics deliver the right results. Failure to understand the difference between the success measures in digital vs. traditional projects has often doomed successful programs before they start.

Experimentation Before Lock-in

The people overseeing healthcare.gov possessed a management philosophy to immediately launch the site and fix it along the way, despite repeated warnings from contractors that more tests and experiments were needed before locking down the strategy and architecture. Businesses use this philosophy as well. Digital provides ample opportunity to test and measure before full commitment. Successful organizations often find new and better strategies throughout this process.

Fortunately, healthcare.gov recovered, thanks to a herculean effort and many revisions. But as discussed, we don't think a business in the world would have either had the resources or time to see an expectations chasm like this through to completion. In fact, when we see much smaller failures, the organization almost always retreats across the board to reevaluate its digital strategies and tactics before jumping back into the water.

Digital Takes Different Metrics

In a digital world where numbers are infinitely available, organizations need to be cognizant of the need to focus on the most valuable metrics, not just the most available. This is a small but significant change that almost anyone who deals with metrics will recognize. In most cases, big, easy numbers like volume metrics look great on reports and tend to help place checkmarks next to quarterly goals. Digital is different. Digital gives organizations the ability to see and use the big, easy numbers as well as the insights and trend indicators that can truly drive competitive aspirations. We have seen numerous client examples where the default is to steer away from big data metrics, even though the business has access to them, and toward traditional and simple reporting of data. The reason for this is usually comfort and conformity with the status quo. After all, it is hard to benchmark with different metrics or educate and convince executives and board members about new measures. One of the ways companies can get around this mentality is to recreate the story for investors by managing the expectations across the company.

> "One of the things I learned at Best Buy is they branded the transformation and called it Renew Blue. They said, 'Here is the profit margin for the business in five years. And here's how brand-new omnichannel growth and e-commerce are going to deliver against it'—and as much as they focused each quarterly report on where we were on same-store sales, they actually took away guidance for each year. They reported against each quarter to focus investors on the multiyear transformation. Reframing the expectations to be multiyear versus short term, branding the change, and holding Best Buy accountable to the nonfinancial metrics associated with long-term performance allowed the investors to buy into the transformation. If you're a

public company and you merely throw your hands up and say, 'Forget about what's happening in the short term. I promise you something good's going to happen,' you're unlikely to have the same degree of freedom. I would say reframing the journey and focusing on the metrics today that predict long-term success versus short-term performance is critical for a transformation."[4]

—David Lee, former SVP, Best Buy

In a digital era, everything is different and changing, and leaders should frequently review their metrics accordingly. The key is to find the right mix of metrics for the group, project, or line of business based on your digital footprint today and in the future. As systems, processes, and businesses change, it is vital that leaders reevaluate what they measure and how they define success.

The most successful economic performers in B2C and B2B categories have four things in common when they think about metrics:

1. Look beyond simple volume metrics.
2. Place equal emphasis on engagement and volume metrics.
3. Track customer abandonment (both unfollowers in social media and cart abandonment in e-commerce) as well as what content and ideas are shared.
4. Care about how advocates are developed and enabled beyond social media, including employees, partners, and customers alike.

The best economic performers let go of simple volume metrics and have a strong metric preference for "perceptual returns."

A synthesis exists between traditional volume metrics, behavioral elements—including activating content, engaging in conversations, speed of reaction, and cart abandonment—and overall perceptions. The fascinating paradox here is that the most successful companies, those that fervently measure, are more than happy handling and rejoicing in the ambiguities of perceptions.

With the near-perfect compression of supply and demand as well as almost infinite access to information for customers, employees, and partners, what we focus on can make or break a business in the digital world. Imagine if your organization is looking at the wrong metrics. If so, you are at best missing clarity and at worst missing meaningful indicators. This is compounded by the competitive nature of most markets where everyone is looking to capitalize on the information at their fingertips. With digital transformation projects growing and the Internet of Things expanding daily, data is becoming more abundant than grains of sand on a beach. Winning organizations will have to continually evolve their metric models to separate the mundane from the significant, giving them long-term benefits for the foreseeable future.

Digital Transformation Perspective

Transforming SanDisk, a twenty-six-year-old, $6.2 billion company, from a successful engineering and sales-oriented culture to a customer-focused culture wasn't a small undertaking. One of the key elements SanDisk discovered was that the correct metrics play a big part in getting digital right.

One of the first lessons was learning what is important to the customer so that they knew what to measure. SanDisk started by determining what was most and least valuable to the customer and their overall satisfaction. SanDisk established relative weights and values for these customer perception metrics and operational KPIs and metrics that correlate to each.

Here is a simple but important example for order management at SanDisk: The company was using the perception metric "rate your experience of our order management on a scale of 1 to 5." When they received low scores, they dug in and found they were really measuring on-time shipments. Customers, on the other hand, cared about on-time delivery. Most of their B2B customers have time windows to receive certain kinds of shipments. If the shipment doesn't arrive within that window it gets scheduled for the next day. When a day is missed, the customer's production is impacted and SanDisk might be forced to pay a penalty. Further analysis found that SanDisk employees were focusing on getting it out the door instead of making sure it arrived when it was supposed to. The bottom line was that what the customer valued had nothing to do with what SanDisk was measuring.

SanDisk's Three Keys to Digital Success

SanDisk transformed into a new, customer-led organization by focusing on three keys:

1. Build a strong sense of ownership across the organization for the program based on the business outcomes that were important to each group.
2. Have a clear link between measurable customer experience metrics and operational metrics.
3. Use quick wins to build trust, credibility, and momentum.

> "We really didn't understand the differences between what each of those customer types needed. When issues cropped up because of those differences, they weren't reported, they were taken care of by individuals on a one-off basis. It's not until you actually start gathering and analyzing data that you realize this is a real problem and a big one that impacts many customers. Problems like these have a material impact on the business and your ability to ramp. Focusing on customer value and experience in a systematic way helps you surface these things."[5]
> —**Reginald Chatman, director of Customer Experience, SanDisk**

Digital Takes a Village and an Architecture

We have said it many times before, but it matters most here: To be successful, any digital transformation effort must deliver a value far in excess of the sum of its parts. Organizations can't just add digital. They need to *be* digital to get the parts working together properly and in the right way. To be greater than the sum of their parts, organizations need a framework to orchestrate all the components, functions, and actions to achieve the promise of digital transformation.

Digital's one true trait is that it touches nearly everything in your organization. As such, digital transformation should be viewed and used as an overriding effort to empower the whole of the organization. Many forget this or focus on the far smaller goal of adding digital inside their group or line of business, but transformation, by definition, means to change in composition or structure, not just to add. It is surprising how many executives forget this concept or try to tackle it alone within a department.

Across the organization, digital must be driven by extremely careful thinking, planning, enablement, metrics, and a constant thirst to push the right boundaries to deliver value beyond just the systems. To further this, we believe that at least 50 percent of your energy must be focused on building buy-in and engagement from key constituents as well as setting up the right architectural elements for governance, council, extensive training, and executive and leadership involvement, among others. The idea of truly isolated experiments in a digital world is not realistic. Digital ecosystems function in a binary manner, and once they start they can grow extremely fast. Starting with a well-thought-out architecture and developing your village enables levels of support and action to springboard and incubate the next digital effort. Without this blueprint in place, digital projects tend to wither or deliver isolated results, never impacting the company as a whole.

> "You can't win the game by buying technology . . . it is as much about human capital and process as it is about the technology you enable people with."
> —**Bruce Rogers, chief insights officer,** *Forbes*

All groups and departments matter in building advocacy. When we look at the factors of possible influence, we can see advocacy is distributed across almost every function. Even if you are not a department immediately affected by the programs, the best organizations understand the need for buy-in and contribution. Not only does the percentage of influence prove winners function best in villages, but it also clearly shows the need to build well-architected systems to win.

Digital Transformation Perspective

Telstra, a major Australian telecom business, had its fixed voice revenue drop from $5.4 billion to $4.4 billion from 2011 to 2013 due in no small part to the mass adoption of mobile devices.

The first key step in its digital transformation was centralizing the existing teams and investments, as the company was spending significant resources on disparate digital platforms. The result was far less value from their investments because of fragmentation in systems and suppliers. The company had five different Internet platforms, five different relationship sets with suppliers, and five different approaches to UX and design. Tasked with bringing them all together, Telstra Digital sourced some of the best digital talent in the market to create one of the most robust digital teams in the country. The move toward one platform and a unified approach to information and channel architecture soon yielded game-changing initiatives.

The Telstra 24x7 smartphone and tablet apps and CrowdSupport community were among them. These helped to revolutionize the way Telstra relates to and services its customers and how they cut the company's cost-to-serve by a significant margin.

> "The benefits were many, but there were also challenges. Some things took longer to implement than we expected. It was important to understand the nuances and the details. We always aimed at the dual benefit of digitizing our systems and processes. This lowered our costs and provided a better customer experience at the same time. Both imperatives fit neatly with our corporate strategy."[6]
>
> **—Gerd Schenkel, executive director, Telstra Digital**

Together their digital efforts created a major channel into the palms of their customers and reduced costs while increasing revenue. The demand for Telstra Digital's services far exceeded supply. "There is a high degree of tech literacy at Telstra," says Schenkel, "which is a good thing. We didn't have to explain too much. But it also meant that everyone wanted more digital functions for their product or their channel."[7]

Success Comes from the Inside Out, Not from the Outside In

The digital era has provided businesses with the ability to scale almost instantly via virtual organizations, cloud deployments, and other outsourcing options. Ironically, successful transformation requires the organization to start with the core digital competency and build out from there. Often a perceived need to catch up or to quickly augment the digital capabilities pushes leaders to outsource key parts of delivery and build. Digital requires the core competency to reside within the organization, and the most successful organizations build the right skills and resources internally first.

> "Reorganization to me is shuffling boxes, moving boxes around. Transformation means that you're really, fundamentally changing the way the organization thinks, the way it responds, the way it leads. It's a lot more than just playing with boxes."[8]
>
> —**Lou Gerstner, legendary former CEO, IBM**

There are two key points leaders need to understand before outsourcing digital:

1. It is critical for the organization to have a core foundation to build on as discussed in all the challenges thus far.
2. Success comes from identifying and augmenting your digital strategy at the right times and with the right parts.

This is a delicate balance but one that is made easy if you have the right architecture and village working together. Our research shows that the most successful organizations invest only about 17 percent of their resources externally. More importantly, these winners focused their outsourcing on a critical set of components that the organization needed to move forward.

To get execution right, you need to facilitate a broad range of internal support defined by advocacy, active engagement, and involvement in the metrics building and assessment. The first failure is to go digital using only the IT department. The most successful organizations worked to get buy-in across nine of eleven departmental functions, including IT, sales, communications, marketing, and others. This is democratization of digital in its most complete way. In fact, the IT function was marginally more critical than other functions like finance and operations for the winners, showing IT alone does not build or start a village.

Failure to recognize the democratization of responsibility is one of the key issues. Leaders cannot build a winning strategy with an outsourced, checkbook mentality. There is a chemistry that is vital to success that includes internal fortitude with wisely chosen external resources.

There are three key points that organizations should be aware of:

1. The distribution of ownership is far greater among the best performers than the least successful.
2. The size of the organization does not matter—from medium to large enterprises, the results remained constant.
3. The capacity to organize these components is a critical element for digital winners.

"If HP only knew what HP knows," former HP executive Lew Platt said, referring to the knowledge that is locked up inside most large organizations.[9]

Openness to Alternative Strategies Drives Digital

Winners in digital relish the data and options transformation provides. The most successful digital and social transformations occur within brands that deliberately design and seek alternative strategies and extensive experimentation before they commit to a full strategy lock-in. This is the beauty and power digital transformation provides.

> "Many executives try to solve the problem of execution by reducing it to a single dimension. They focus on tightening alignment up and down the chain of command—by improving existing processes, such as strategic planning and performance management."[10]
>
> —**Donald Sull, Rebecca Homkes, and Charles Sull**

As we have discussed, the amount and pace of change is an opportunity to become a new winner or to fall behind. The difference between rising or falling is often an organization's ability to identify and capitalize on the opportunities that appear. To do so requires an agile approach to strategy and a willingness to experiment to see what will pan out. Many of the organizations that have lost their standing have fallen victim to either being too rigid in their strategy or being unwilling to take risks and experiment.

Think about former leaders who stuck to their guns and, as a result, have either failed or are slowly sliding away:

- Nokia had the ecosystem, patents, technology, and capital to compete with virtually anyone, but they did not react fast enough to the software and usability advances Apple and Google brought to the market.

- Quiznos practically reinvented the sandwich restaurant category by toasting its subs but failed to see how price was becoming a differentiator, especially during the recession, and now has reduced its stores by 40 percent. On the other hand, Subway is growing at a record pace, thanks to its $5 and $6 specials on their footlong sandwiches, health focus, and also now toasting its subs.

- Groupon has struggled to stem the loss of market share and profits while trying to compete with more than a hundred big and small "deal sites." The company, which grew at meteoric proportions leading up to its IPO in 2011, failed to see that consumers were more interested in finding a deal on what they were buying at the time of purchase rather than seeing a collection of deals advertised.

The companies listed above are not ones that missed technology shifts like Blockbuster did with online video or Kodak did with digital photography. Rather, these organizations missed market and consumer shifts, causing them to go from being market leaders to a fraction of their former standing. The market is speaking and sending signs for these shifts every minute of every day and in a number of ways. Digital transformation, when fully implemented, is the engine and driver to uncover and leverage these signals. It is a brand's job to use its village and read the tea leaves across a myriad of functions and determine where to experiment, where to shift, and when to abandon its strategy. Not one of the companies listed above was without warning or did not have the resources to experiment and identify new growth paths.

In addition to identifying the changes, digital needs to also deliver new social and digital transformative programs twice as fast. This requires collaboration. But one of the key tenets of rewarding employees and managers is their past performance. Their past efforts and successes are two or three times more likely to be rewarded with a promotion than a track record of collaboration. Not only does this run counter to the needs of a holistic digital transformation, but it also presents barriers to trying, failing, and offering alternative strategies up front.

Organizations need to understand that strategy lock-in occurs on both a micro and macro level. There are dozens of examples inside your organization where individuals or teams have fallen into the trap of trying to infinitely scale successes in execution. While not as catastrophic as inflexible organization-wide strategy, this fallacy still locks the business into a path that pushes leaders to ignore potentially enriching new avenues. We see this type of pattern often once a successful platform or system has been discovered. For example, brands that experience success marketing on YouTube or see how Eloqua was successfully generating more digital marketing returns tend to put all of their eggs into these baskets. It is understandable to pursue maximum returns and to keep going toward the action or tactic that is working.

However, in a digital world the question is, when are you maximizing returns vs. locking in a strategy that excludes other options? Winners in digital transformation are extremely aware of the need to push boundaries in one or many areas of the business, knowing they need to find the "next thing" to drive further success. The key is to accept that each form of digital (sales, marketing, social, HR, etc.) may have a threshold or ceiling for results. The best brands and performers recognize the need for a near complete and growing set of transformative options and investments to drive success. The best brands and performers seek not only new platforms and systems but also, more importantly, new uses and angles different from what they have already. This can include almost any kind of experiment across any function, such as social, marketing, products, services, sales, support, and much more.

One of the best ways to determine how to maximize returns or how to lock in a strategy is to first ask three questions around any problem area:

1. What should we stop doing?
2. What should we start doing?
3. What should we do differently?

These questions will help frame the problem in a better way than simply deciding or locking in a strategy. Another dangerous pitfall is when a team prematurely develops a bias for action. This risk is particularly acute among managers who pride themselves on getting the job done. The result: the team shortchanges the "what if" discussion and jumps right into a debate about how to do it. If the conversation rushes too quickly through the messy thrashing around of sense making and questioning the alternative, managers risk diving into the details of implementation before they've explored alternative assessments, surfaced and checked key assumptions, or tested the fit between their interpretation and the facts on the ground.

Digital Transformation Perspective

Perhaps no other organization is as innovative or attempts more experiments than Google. Have you ever wondered what makes Google the holy grail of productivity and creativity? The company focuses its efforts on nine core principles of innovation:

1. Innovation comes from anywhere. It can come from the top down as well as bottom up, and from the places you least expect.
2. Focus on the user. Worry about the money later. When you focus on the user, all else will follow.
3. Aim to be ten times better. If you come into work thinking that you will improve things by 10 percent, you will only see incremental

change. If you want radical and revolutionary innovation, think ten times improvement, and that will force you to think outside the box.

4. Bet on technical insights. Every organization has unique insights, and if you bet on them, they lead to major innovation. For example, Google engineers, not the auto industry, came up with the idea of driverless cars after seeing that millions of traffic deaths result from human error.

5. Ship and iterate. Ship your products often and early, and do not wait for perfection. Let users help you to iterate it.

6. Give employees 20 percent time. Give employees 20 percent of their work time to pursue projects they are passionate about, even if the projects are outside the core job or core mission of the company.

7. Default to open processes. Make your processes open to all users. Tap into the collective energy of the user base to obtain great ideas.

8. Fail well. There should be no stigma attached to failure. If you do not fail often, you are not trying hard enough.

9. Have a mission that matters. Everyone should have a strong sense of mission and purpose, and each person should have his or her own story.[11]

Just think of the long list of experiments and alternative strategies that have become successes from these principles:

- Blogger—jump-started the blogging revolution by making it free
- Google Translate—free translations across sixty-four languages
- Google Docs—free "Office-like" productivity tools
- Google Chrome—one of the leading Web browsers
- Android—350 million smart devices and growing
- Google Maps—almost single-handedly killing the GPS market
- Gmail—free, unlimited email storage

Remember, this company started out as a search engine business. Now Google touches almost every element of our digital lives. Their methods for innovation are to credit as much as the superior products they have delivered. But don't forget Google's failures! Google has had more than its share of disasters, including Google Buzz, Google Plus, and Google Wave, among others.

> "Google's failure rate is higher than 95 percent in some cases. This is a company where it's absolutely okay to try something that's very hard, have it not be successful, and learn from that."[12]
> —Eric Schmidt, former CEO, Google

Digital Is Not Just Customer Focused

There is no doubt digital was made for delivering customer-focused results. After all, customer feedback accelerated exponentially with social, and this is a big driver for the overall digital transition phase we are in now. Despite its customer benefits, far too many organizations limit the power and efficacy of digital to just this one area of the business.

It is essential for organizations to be obsessed with the customer and relentlessly evolve and improve the customer experience. However, many organizations fail to realize the digital investments required to pay off the customer-centric vision. In fact, there are numerous examples where back-office functions delivered far more than customer-facing ones. P&G collaborated with the Los Alamos National Laboratory to create statistical methods to streamline processes and increase uptime at its factories. The result: P&G saved more than $1 billion a year.

This, too, is the power of digital to transform business processes and functions that can create a competitive advantage. P&G is now more efficient and can produce either more cost-effective products or run at higher margins than its competitors. This, in many ways, is far more disruptive than being more customer-centric. The key is to follow the money and identify ways to use digital to reduce costs. When done right, digital can knock down the barriers and hurdles that rob value from the business.

> "I'll keep you in the right direction if I can, but that's all. Just . . . follow the money."
> —Deep Throat, in the film *All the President's Men*

There are two factors that tend to cause failure and should be avoided. Leaders must recognize that some or even all Seven Challenges will affect your organization at some point. It is too easy to focus on the desired outcome and miss the challenge or challenges that are presenting themselves. This usually pushes leaders to immediately jump to actions and tactics without ever identifying and fixing the root cause. Without addressing the challenge, your organization cannot hope to ever achieve its full digital transformation potential.

The second failing is assuming that your infrastructure investments cannot be scaled to provide value across other investments and areas of the business. This is a major issue for isolated decision-making. The same is true when we look at digitally enabling technologies. For example, if your group is primarily using Eloqua, Marketo, Salesforce, or another software package for one area of the business, other parts of the internal ecosystem will need, at the very least, to understand how it affects them in terms of information coming in, decisions being made, or even processes needing to change. It's not just the act of implementing more types of digital infrastructure that matters. It is the success in using support and executive engagement across functions and the ability to review and develop new business processes. For transformation to work, the organization needs active buy-in from all departments across all functions, from design to metrics. Failure to build that ecosystem stunts the capacity of the technologies and the people involved to fully transform digitally.

> "We're in the midst of an evolutionary adaptation in which people are being forced to gate out irrelevant information. And we're in a time-compressed, rapid-paced life and business environment. With information flooding our visual and vestibular systems in our brains, those that can gate out irrelevant information, be present with a fast-moving environment, will have a competitive advantage. To succeed, we need to train people's minds to be in chaotic environments and to listen better and differently."
> — **Dr. Michael Gervais, consultant to world-class athletes and teams, cofounder, Compete To Create Consulting**

Digital Transformation Perspective

In 2009, after dismal performance cut the company's stock price in half, Starbucks looked to digital to help re-engage with customers and improve the bottom line. Starbucks' chief digital officer and chief information officer formed a close working relationship and restructured their teams so that they could collaborate from the very start of projects. In 2013, they reduced time-in-line by nine hundred thousand hours, cutting ten seconds from every card or mobile phone transaction. In addition, Starbucks has added mobile payment processing to its stores, processing three million mobile payments per week. While all of this benefits customers, it is the back-office functions that have improved and transformed to make the business as a whole better.[13]

It All Seems Connected in Some Way

Of all the challenges we have discussed in this chapter, there is one common theme—digital has to be built from the core of the business to succeed. Leaders who look at digital transformation as an incremental step or process tend to fail. Even experiments and new digital additions need to be made on a bedrock foundation consisting of—

1. Executive action and involvement
2. Understanding and realistic communication of the achievable results
3. Realization that what is measured must matter and demonstrate value
4. Deep buy-in, support, and resources on top of the right architecture
5. Internal understanding before external resources are added
6. Flexible strategies matched with experiments to identify and leverage the shifts that occur
7. Appreciation for the holistic value digital can bring across the business

Winning with digital is not easy. But it is fundamentally made simpler and more repeatable once leaders understand how these challenges sabotage their efforts. The key is to see the combination of what to avoid (unforced errors) as well as the fundamentals of how to do digital right as an imperative for corporate high performance.

> "As a multisport athlete, I was always fascinated with competition and how to win. At HBS and later at the Harvard Department of Economics, I was drawn to the field of competition and strategy because it tackles perhaps the most basic question in both business management and industrial economics: What determines corporate performance?"[14]
>
> **—Michael Porter, professor, Harvard Business School**

We believe that these Seven Challenges should be driving how you think about digital transformation and set up your organization to win in the long run. Yet businesses need to address and overcome these challenges before moving full speed into a transformation effort. Far too often a company's first move is to reorganize and then add digital. The key is that organizations need to be digital first. Can you point to initiatives and efforts in your organization that have broken with the principles of the digital best practices?

CHAPTER 6

SMALL STEPS EQUAL GIANT LEAPS

"The world as we have created it is a process of our thinking. It cannot be changed without changing our thinking."
—Albert Einstein

From our research and conversations with digital transformation leaders, we have found that an organization's ability to recognize the key drivers and barriers that impact success is more than half the battle for winning with digital. The issue, as we have stated, becomes identifying which drivers and challenges affect your organization from the hundreds of possible combinations. In reality there are too many permutations to solve for all of them, but there is a place to start. One of the keys used by successful organizations is that they start by framing the debate and discussion around digital transformation projects. Modifying how you discuss digital transformation and its concepts changes how the organization navigates its next steps and realigns its priorities.

The amount of time leaders invest in digital transformation is immense. In the research we conducted, one of the more remarkable facts was how much time leaders believe they will spend every week on digital transformation inside their organization, now and three years into the future. Finding any way to make digital transformation easier or better is crucial. Having a digital framework for the projects as well as the concepts and how they are discussed leads to real transformative thinking. It may seem a little ridiculous that such a small change could have such a big impact, but if the goal is to get people moving in a new direction, you need to introduce a new way of thinking. And this new way of thinking requires executives to spend more time in the future to bring the organization into alignment with new digital directives and initiative, as you will see from our research in figure 6.1.

> "You never change things by fighting the existing reality. To change something, build a new model that makes the existing model obsolete."[1]
> **—Buckminster Fuller, American architect, systems theorist, author, designer, and inventor**

From our research on transformation, we can see the significant time investment leaders are putting into their digital efforts both now and in the future.

DIGITAL TRANSFORMATION PERSPECTIVE

From ICF digital research, we can see the significant time investment leaders are putting into their transformation efforts:

IN THE NEXT 12 MONTHS	OVER THE NEXT 3 YEARS
Leaders estimate they will spend an average of **19.9 hours** per person, per week on digital transformation issues	The average will rise to **22 hours** per person, per week spent on digital transformation issues

Figure 6.1: How Leaders See Time Investments in Digital Transformation

This shift in thinking and language is an inspiring idea, but one that may fill your team with dread. Part of moving to this more digital state requires the team and organization to provide more than best efforts. Successful organizations work to have a love affair with their own digital transformation process and celebrate each achievement. Having this level of affinity with your digital transformation is virtually impossible if organization members keep trying to equate everything to an extension or simple evolution of your existing state. This "backward compatibility" thinking not only limits dialogue but also prevents the team and organization from pushing the digital limits.

> "I think the shifts that are occurring are both coming from the outside and from within. The drivers are the expectations that people have and see wherever they go. People, whether they are in the role of buyers or citizens, expect an 'Amazonian' experience. When they see one or two organizations, or even internal groups, delivering at this higher digital level, they expect everyone to provide an experience that is equal to or better. This expectation one-upmanship is the driver pushing all of us to do better."
>
> —**Gwynne Kostin, senior advisor, GSA Technology Transformation Service**

To get beyond these artificial concept and language barriers, organizations must understand three key shifts in thinking (both at the employee and organization level):

1. Making giant leaps requires new concepts. New ideas and concepts matter in this digital world. We can't use mainly old-world ideas or words to describe new-world mindsets. Language is a vital ingredient in any transformative process and even more so in one transforming so fast. If organizations want to change behaviors and performance, they need to gravitate toward new digital concepts to see and understand where the opportunities lie.

2. Small changes are the key to long-term results. Because digital transformation requires the investment of so much of it, time is one of our greatest potential assets. But the lack of time can also be a huge liability for effective performance. The key to getting time back and prioritizing is sometimes as simple as asking the right questions within the right framework. As we will discuss in detail later in the chapter, one key exercise we have used to help get time back within a group or organization is called Stop/Start/Do Differently, a method that has proven to provide dramatic results. Quite simply, you ask what can you stop, start, or do differently across key aspects of the business.

3. Success breeds success. In digital transformation, as in other endeavors across the organization, gaining momentum and having success drives more and more results. There are a number of functional as well as psychological reasons for this. In a category where about one in seven are struggling to deliver real results, having just a little taste of victory can cause ripples across the organization. This is another reason why we are highlighting the little things in this chapter.

Language and barriers seem like simple things to overcome. When aiming to deliver real results in digital, overcoming these simple hurdles is often what separates your organization from those that struggle.

> "Once you get into the digital mode and have shifted out of the old way into the new way, you realize that it's very empowering. You can make huge leaps when everyone sees what is possible and says, 'Let's go after it. Let's do it right. Let's build something to be proud of.'"
> —**Greg Godbout, cofounder and CEO, cBrain North America**

Making Giant Leaps Requires New Concepts

We need to be clear. Digital has the power to revolutionize your organization. One of the biggest failures organizations make is shooting too low. Organizations that don't fully move their thinking to digital—whether in strategy, concepts, or language—risk underdelivering and underperforming. This is not about digitally wrapping old-world language into the new world.

Think about it like this: When your organization moved to take advantage of social and Web 2.0, did you keep thinking and talking about these shifts in traditional terms? Or did you use the new language and concepts that came with the shift because they were clearer and provided much more depth in meaning? In the same way terms such as "content," "touches," and "journey" mean specific things in the social and Web 2.0 worlds, the new digital world has its own concepts that provide greater clarity and meaning.

> "Words matter here. We spend a lot of time discussing how we talk about driving digital transformation within our business. More specifically, we are a relationship company with a focus on digital capabilities to meet the needs and expectations of our members. This is no longer about reaching a destination but will be a perpetual journey that will continuously evolve. We're always trying to get better at describing what being a digital enterprise or digital-first organization means in the context of better serving our members in the most dynamic, personalized, and contextual way possible."
>
> —**Chris Cox, head of Digital Experience Delivery, USAA**

Digital Transformation Perspective

In the digital era, concepts, thinking, and language help drive transformative change. Figure 6.2 lists key digital transformation shifts that can help drive success.

Figure 6.2: How Concepts Are Changing from the Old to the New World

When you look at the concepts above, some of the changes may sound or appear to be semantic in nature. They are not. Look at a few of these in detail below. As you read each, try to recognize that every concept shift drives a noticeable change in the way we need to think, collaborate, and act.

1. **Reach to engagement levels**: Reach is about a moment, one where we claim we have touched an audience. The key is to think about the broader scope of the term "reach," beyond the association with media. Reach does and should affect all communications and touches. Engagement, on the other hand, is about the exchange of value. As many organizations have figured out, engagement is focused on the nature and quality of the dialogue rather than the volume. But in the digital era "engagement" is a pervasive and all-encompassing term. In this form, engagement goes beyond marketing and communications

to sales, support, delivery, and billing. In short, it is the total sum of a brand's interactions with the consumer that should ideally lead to evangelism, if done correctly and consistently.

2. **Metrics to insights that drive decisions that matter**: We live in a big data, numbers-rich world, but that does not always mean we know or focus on the right insights. "Metrics" is often seen as a term about gathering information. But successful organizations blend volume with value in the right proportions. Yes, getting more customers is a good measure, but more important is understanding how to get more of the right or better customers for future growth.

3. **Average customer to leading customers**: If you focus on the average customer or only on key groups of customers, you run the risk of missing future potential. In a fast-evolving world, we cannot assume that our customer base will not change or that the change will happen over many months or years. Almost all new and emerging leaders that replaced industry stalwarts did so by serving the leading customer as we previously discussed (taxis to Uber, Quiznos to Subway, etc.). This type of failing in the Digital Age is inexcusable, as any business can see nearly every aspect of a customer. The key is to mine customer insights while looking for potential future customers.

4. **Historical performance to real-time insights**: Hindsight is not a logical singular lens for transformation. Since historical measures are easy, corporations often struggle with this. In a digital world that is constantly changing, it is critical to look at all the right views to get the best information and ultimately the answers. As your industry and others leverage digital, competition increases. Therefore, winners will be the ones using all available data to plot the newest and best paths, and losers will be wasting time looking in the wrong places. Insights come from social, sales, brand feedback, competitors, shifting trends, customer data, support data, trending conversations, and more. As a leader, you need to focus on the range of views and insights as well as the right moment to apply these learnings.

5. **Create content to cocreated content**: In the rush to get out brand information and become their own media firm, organizations often go it alone with a volume-is-better mentality. The bar is usually set

rather low as organizations see how much of their story they can get out while trying to garner some level of engagement. Just because brands have the power to publish does not mean they have the content to engage. There needs to be a shift in the way we think about content. In advertising, like in content, ideas and creative power rule. (This was father of advertising David Ogilvy's mantra.) When you set quotas but want to first tell a story, your initial steps are in reverse. Engagement comes from showing you are the right company that is doing the right things worthy of engagement. Thinking digitally about content first requires a focus on the ideas and conversation occurring and what the audience wants. Together with the power of crowds and partners you can create a vital mechanism for driving interest and brand evangelism.

Small Changes Are the Key to Long-term Results

As discussed, in digital transformation many times the little things are what matter the most. Metrics, coordination, expectations, and other simple and small pieces have a tremendous effect on the ultimate success or failure of a project. This is not to say you have to do everything right. The point is that the small things add up, and missing a few steps makes it tougher to recover. Conversely, getting a few right from the start gives you breathing room when things do go sideways. The key is that leaders and teams need to spend as much time and energy on the small parts of digital transformation efforts as the large ones.

> "With digital, we can make small changes in real time. It gives us much more granular measures to see changes much more frequently while efforts are underway. Now, we can make a small change in a business process, campaign, or any activity to optimize the result immediately. These small, ongoing changes are the keys to getting better results and driving long-term digital results."
>
> —Lisa Macpherson, CMO/SVP of marketing, Hallmark

Far too often, teams push to gain momentum and critical mass with much speed to overcome organizational inertia. It can be seen in the initial stages of any project when questions like these dominate the discussions:

- Do we have enough people behind this?
- Do we have enough results now to go faster?
- Do we have a successful formula we can scale with?

If you remember back to the Seven Challenges, these are not the things that trip up digital transformation efforts. These are management issues that naturally arise with this effort. Navigating from one segment of digital transformation readiness or performance to another is a tricky activity because it involves an underlying set of assumptions and behaviors that can hurt you. Think about the following four erroneous assumptions and whether they affect your organization:

1. **Go short term**: Looking for the next quick win sounds logical. But the research we conducted on digital transformation reveals that 58 percent of leaders in successful corporations say planning a longer-term strategy is more important than short-term goals (4 percent). The critical point is that digital transformation is a building process where each piece either builds on the next or connects to the old. Long-term success requires you to think many moves ahead or become stuck with disparate tools and technologies.

2. **Do more of the same**: Being open to looking through a different lens beyond what you are doing is vital. Even though digital is infinitely scalable, each activity or project is not. Doing more of the same seems like a safe bet, but it should be your last choice, not your first. To thrive, digital has to permeate throughout the organization. Loading up on select projects means you are probably missing others while facing diminishing returns on the ones you are milking now.

3. **There is only one next step**: As we talked about with the Seven Challenges, developing alternative strategies is critical for success. Using all views, not just a rear view, to design your future direction is vital.

As we have seen in our interviews and research, successful firms seek the best paths and try out many before locking in a flexible strategy for digital transformation. This approach has led many organizations to getting multiple wins simultaneously with their efforts, as well as fallback positions should one not deliver.

4. **It feels simple, so let's leap**: In our research on successful digital transformations, we asked executives and leaders if complexity caused issues. Thirty-seven percent of respondents said they lacked information around the unforeseen levels of complexity involved in the process. This was a key point for those who reported below-average results as well. As we have discussed, many times you don't know what you don't know, and understanding and building the right foundation is critical to your organization's long-term success.

Master Time to Manage Successful Transformations

Time and resources are precious. Understanding and incorporating new concepts across the organization drives intent and agreement on outcomes as well as next steps that can drive or hinder longer-term success. To get this right, you need to recognize that there are aspects of the business and daily work you need to stop or do differently.

> "Whether you are a startup, a large corporation, an individual athlete, or a collective team, human performance depends on one of our most precious and fragile resources: time. So, if we can really get our arms around this idea that time, meaning this moment, is our most precious resource, we are likely to struggle and not perform at our best. Time is the vehicle in which we experience life and relationships and where performance is expressed. So if we can help our individual performers increase the quality and frequency in which they experience moments, then we're going to have a dramatic increase in output."
>
> —**Dr. Michael Gervais, consultant to world-class athletes and teams, cofounder, Compete To Create Consulting**

The insights below cover the four areas we recommend you use. Additionally, there are four facts and reasons why you need to do this exercise, based on the research from our digital transformation work:

- 34 percent of digital transformation activities have not met the expected results. Only 21 percent exceeded expectations.
- 32 percent of executives argue that failure to respond or react to startups in the next two years is greater than today. We need to find ways to do things differently in order to respond better.
- 40 percent of executives told us that if they are not fully digitally transformed in three years, they will not be highly competitive.

On the more positive side, executives and leaders believed that ideas including near real-time products, the wider access to information that customers have, and the new match of innovation and efficiency are opportunities more than threats on a 3:1 ratio.

Telling your teams or organizations to be better with time is wholly insufficient. If they could be more efficient, they would. As leaders, we need to identify the organizational issues and processes that rob time from our people and teams. In far too many cases, this is a collection of tasks and tactics that once identified can either be removed or greatly truncated.

One solution is the Stop/Start/Do Differently method. As we mentioned earlier, you simply ask what you can stop, start, or do differently throughout the business. The key is to use a framework like the one that follows to find the time and effort wasters across—

1. Relationships and interactions
2. Resources and allocations
3. Questions and focus
4. Outcomes and activities

With this framework and the following instructions, you will be able to identify the key elements that drag down productivity and waste time.

Digital Transformation Tools

THE STOP/START/DO DIFFERENTLY EXERCISE

As mentioned, the secret to getting time back and prioritizing your team's or group's efforts is to ask the right questions within the right framework. This simple exercise is designed to help you do just that while enabling you to achieve dramatic results. We have used this exercise numerous times with our clients, and in every case it has yielded insights that have improved productivity and focus. The secret is to work with a small group of colleagues on one major digital transformation issue at a time.

This works best in a conference or large room where each team member can use Post-It notes to share their thoughts. We recommend using a different color for each of the four topics above. The leader should make sure that as a group, equal attention is placed on what to stop, start, or do differently. The key is for teams to give up and/or modify something in the end before adding a new item as time and resources are scarce.

Use these ten questions to get started:

Relationships and interactions:
1. Which relationships matter?
2. How do we change these interactions (with each relevant group or person)?
3. What do we do with current or new relationships?

Resources and allocations:
4. Which resources do we use?
5. How do we handle the allocations?
6. What should we do internally and with external partners?

Questions and focus:
7. Which ones do we ask?
8. What are the right focuses for us on this challenge?

Outcomes and activities:
9. How do we measure success?
10. Which outcomes matter?

Use or create a version of the chart below and have everyone post his or her thoughts in the appropriate sections. (A larger version of this chart below is available at TheDigitalHelix.com.)

	STOP	START	DO DIFFERNTLY
Relationships & Interactions			
Resources & Allocations			
Questions & Focus			
Outcomes & Activities			

Figure 6.3: The Stop/Start/Do Differently Exercise

There are five takeaways you want to get out of this exercise based on the experience of doing this with hundreds of C-level and departmental leaders:

1. Focus on the stop items first. As mentioned, you cannot just add more digital and be successful. As the leader, you need to be prepared to remove new items and should push to have at least 30 percent of your final items fall under stops.
2. The "Questions and focus" category is the most important area for most organizations because it drives how you collaborate and design your future. Spend 50 percent of your time in this section, and you may want to start here when discussing the team's thoughts.
3. Be prepared to come up with a clear action list of three to five items to rally the team and focus efforts. Ideally, you should allocate teams to each key item and provide them with additional time to affect changes and coordination. Do not make this an optional add-on to their workloads or it will not happen.
4. Narrow down the suggestions and thoughts, as many of these will probably fit into similar issues and ideas. As you do so, build consensus with the group on the final ideas, categories, and solutions.
5. Get the final list of ideas that the team agrees are most important and will deliver the greatest impact. Publish the list in the chart above so colleagues can see the process. The list will show the range of insights, but more importantly, it will stimulate their thinking and help get others involved in the project.

Success Breeds Success

In our recent digital transformation research report, we discovered that just a little taste of victory in digital transformation can propel more success for organizations. The numbers are compelling across a vast array of business criteria. Here are a few of the findings:

- Organizations that spend more than $2 million a year on digital transformation are three times more likely to exceed expectations.

- Businesses increasing their focus on digital transformation in the next twelve months were twice as likely to exceed expectations.
- 57 percent of digital leaders said success enabled them to greatly expand digital efforts.
- 49 percent of digital leaders reported that digital helped the organization integrate new technologies to improve business results.
- 49 percent said digital success helped them identify and solve key problems they were not yet focused on.

It is not surprising that success breeds more success. The key is that success in digital accelerates success and growth while springboarding more digital projects. As these statistics show, success is due to the combination of digital transformation delivering on its promise to drive efficiency as well as helping to identify new areas of improvement.

The true promise of digital transformation is to remove the trade-offs between cost, efficiency, and innovation. Leaders who architected for digital success saw and continue to see the results snowball as technology, teams, and the organization find value and build on it. Organizations that saw less than expected or no success found themselves battling against the expectations, metrics, architecture, and other challenges. This, unsurprisingly, led to a pullback in digital and a reevaluation of the process. How have leaders reacted when digital projects hit road bumps in your organization, and do you think they could have been handled differently?

PART 3

THE DIGITAL FRAMEWORK FOR SUCCESS

CHAPTER 7

THE DIGITAL HELIX: AN INTRODUCTION

"If you want to understand function, study structure."
—Francis Crick, codiscoverer, with James Watson, of
the structure of the DNA molecule in 1953

History teaches us that retrofitting only goes so far. Every generational shift has involved trying to retrofit historical ways of thinking and acting into a new world. Roads built for horses were patched to work for cars. Sailboats were given copper bottoms and retrofitted with steam engines to speed them up to compete. At a certain point, retrofitting wasn't enough. Steam ships were completely redesigned to surpass anything a retrofitted sailboat could do. Cars became far too powerful for dirt-paved roads built for horses, so highways were built. The same is true of the digital promise. Retrofitting can only get you so far. At some point, you need to think and act differently in order to take full advantage of all the promises laid out by the Digital Age. Success for brands like Amazon, Google, Facebook, and others shows how digital-first thinking drives exceptional results.

"The people that are most likely to get, understand, accept, and even embrace what digital transformation can mean are people who take history seriously. These people take the future seriously, because they can understand intellectually what history and situational awareness mean to the economic means of production, the economics and the cost associated with them, and change itself."

—**Michael Schrage, research fellow at MIT Sloan School's Initiative on the Digital Economy, oversees research on digital experimentation and network effects, and is author of** *The Innovator's Hypothesis*

Social Media Shows Us the Gap between Retrofitting and Architecting for Success

In an age increasingly dominated by a digital-first mentality in design and delivery, many corporations have tried to retrofit themselves into a new age: technology infrastructure, culture, skills, metrics, and even more importantly, go-to-market communications and marketing. Maybe the best example of this is the social media revolution we are seeing inside this digital migration.

Few, if any, executives and senior managers of Fortune 1000–level corporations would disagree that social media, when done right, can inspire constituents and deliver true, long-term value to organizations. In fact, 87 percent of executives are positive about the potential of social media as a marketing and communication tool.[1] However, when we measured across eight separate economic impact metrics and more than twenty separate types of social media engagement, only 16 percent of Fortune-level corporations believed they had sustained strong economic returns. Between 2012 and 2013 the gap between those doing social media right and those trying to retrofit social media with old ways of thinking and acting ballooned. In 2012, the winners were four times more successful than the losers. In 2013, the gap went to eight to one. The winners doubled the gap because they got social media right from a thinking, infrastructure, and execution process.

Winners Have Unique DNA

The analogy of retrofitting sailboats or of paving horse roads for cars makes sense here because we have tipped past the point where retrofitting our organizations to win at digital makes logical sense. Initially, one might have been able to become a little faster, and retrofitting might have been able to keep an organization from falling too far behind. But in the Digital Age, organizations need to build from the ground up to have any real shot at competing and winning.

Almost without exception, business leaders said digital matters, but it must be done right to yield results. The promise of embracing digital in the right way can be seen by the 16 percent who get exceptional results from their social media strategy and execution. We have discovered there are combinations of elements, like DNA, that are key indicators for success. In digital, the elements are behaviors, organizational design, tactical focus, and even metrics models that differentiate from one group to the next. Much like DNA, seemingly miniscule differences in an organization's DNA lead to dramatically different and, in some cases, better results. To use the ship analogy again, the very act of designing without thinking about a huge mainsail showed and enabled dramatic changes in architecture, intent, and capabilities of steam ships.

> "The DNA of all organizations is changing, and increasingly, the ways that we demarcate between big and small, commercial and nonprofit, and government and citizens are blurring. Ultimately, the organizations that will be most successful are hybrids that identify the best approaches, regardless of domain, and then work to empower their workers with the kind of mission and passion needed to both excite their stakeholders and deliver meaningful results."
> —**David Bray, CIO, Federal Communications Commission**

Reimagining what a great ship should look like and how it could behave was key for success during shipping's transformation. Similarly, building great road systems for cars looked quite different from building great roads for horses and carriages. Effectively, the shape of solution was substantially different from one generation to the next.

> "Virtually everybody's transforming, but only half of the organizations and their leaders know what they're transforming from and to. But every C-level leader and board wants to be there. But to get there, you have to master digital channels, data and analytics, social; create a culture of transparency; develop internal capabilities to implement; and then, leverage all the opportunities they bring. And then, at the end of that discussion, hopefully, is the technology discussion. But with all of this you need a framework to bring it and keep it all together. Without getting everything set up right to build and use the transformation to grow and win, organizations just take a leap of faith on a road that is headed down an enviable digital path. And that is a scary proposition."
> —**Bruce Rogers, chief insights officer,** *Forbes*

The Digital Helix Was Born

Research shows us that there are seven key elements that describe what most successful digital organizations focus on and prioritize. These include world-class digital marketing and communications, product development, and service and support, all working in concert with each other. In addition, successful and truly digital organizations have everybody working together and responsible to each other since insights and information must be connected to deliver for the customer. These seven key elements of the Digital Helix are interconnected to provide the lens from which customer, product, organizational design, marketing, and sales decisions should be made.

They are:

1. In the successful digital organization, the executive is not simply the navigator and mapmaker for the corporation. The executive needs to

The Digital Helix: An Introduction   109

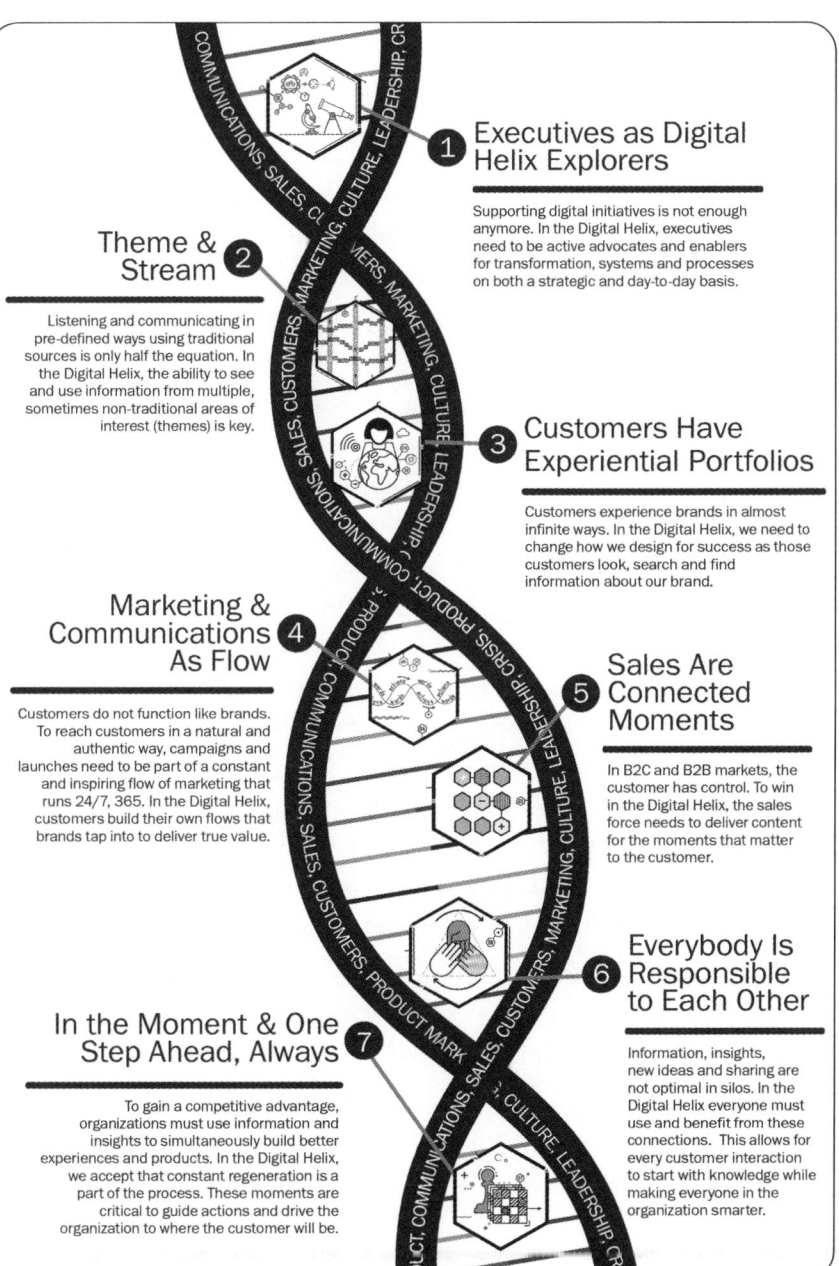

Figure 7.1: The Digital Helix

1. Executives as Digital Helix Explorers

Supporting digital initiatives is not enough anymore. In the Digital Helix, executives need to be active advocates and enablers for transformation, systems and processes on both a strategic and day-to-day basis.

2. Theme & Stream

Listening and communicating in pre-defined ways using traditional sources is only half the equation. In the Digital Helix, the ability to see and use information from multiple, sometimes non-traditional areas of interest (themes) is key.

3. Customers Have Experiential Portfolios

Customers experience brands in almost infinite ways. In the Digital Helix, we need to change how we design for success as those customers look, search and find information about our brand.

4. Marketing & Communications As Flow

Customers do not function like brands. To reach customers in a natural and authentic way, campaigns and launches need to be part of a constant and inspiring flow of marketing that runs 24/7, 365. In the Digital Helix, customers build their own flows that brands tap into to deliver true value.

5. Sales Are Connected Moments

In B2C and B2B markets, the customer has control. To win in the Digital Helix, the sales force needs to deliver content for the moments that matter to the customer.

6. Everybody Is Responsible to Each Other

Information, insights, new ideas and sharing are not optimal in silos. In the Digital Helix everyone must use and benefit from these connections. This allows for every customer interaction to start with knowledge while making everyone in the organization smarter.

7. In the Moment & One Step Ahead, Always

To gain a competitive advantage, organizations must use information and insights to simultaneously build better experiences and products. In the Digital Helix, we accept that constant regeneration is a part of the process. These moments are critical to guide actions and drive the organization to where the customer will be.

go beyond and become an active explorer of the new frontier to discover all the possibilities. Digital done right means embracing the need for constant learning and ongoing experimentation and enabling the organization to succeed at the nodal level. Executives need to lead by example and not just dictate. We call these executives "Digital Helix explorers." Explorers see things at both the micro and macro levels and should flourish in multiple dimensions, when given the opportunity, while constantly strategizing for their organization's actions. They see the world as a series of adjustments and not just a center of command and control. They use digital tools to move quickly, see below the surface, and react swiftly to changing conditions.

2. Information flows in connected ways both horizontally and vertically across the organization. Knowledge is gained from constant interactions with customers and the market. This sharing and transfer of information enables value and creates opportunities that are often left by the wayside in traditional organizations. We refer to this seamless and pervasive use of insights as themes and streams. Digital Helix organizations see information as two intertwined flows—inputs and outputs—which are consciously searched for but randomly found. These flows are no longer contradictions or torsions but synchronous processes. The goal is to find key streams where they matter and become relevant while learning to back off and adjust when they lose relevance. Information is a constantly evolving landscape that needs to be remapped continually so that users can focus only on what is needed and not become overwhelmed by the noise.

3. Marketing has seen that customers have various and differing interactions. Some consumers can be directly driven and guided, but others require the ability to react. Some even focus only on listening, learning from, and utilizing those interactions throughout the organization. We refer to this collective customer interaction as the experiential portfolios of customers. Organizations should know everything customers have in their portfolio of experiences but understand that only certain aspects of the portfolio can be owned, rented, or acted on by the organization. The new goal of a Digital Helix organization's marketing is to build each of these experiences into a collection of inspiring brand moments. Historically,

the analog method was designed to blindly sell, ignore, or resolve the transaction with each interaction. In the Digital Age, enhancing, rewarding, and enriching become the new goals for interactions. Digital tools and ideas enable us to see, understand, and act in near real time and use the customer's own experiences to help build value for their portfolio.

4. Marketing and communications professionals tend to focus a lot on journeys, campaigns, and programs. However, the digital-first customer lives in flows of information and virtual experiences across multiple devices. Organizations that attempt to be part of this flow and seek to learn how to navigate the individual's interactive cycle see more return than old-style entities that rely on trying to interrupt the customer mindset with a campaign, program, or by simply responding. We call this "using marketing and communications as a flow." Marketing should no longer be a single moment but instead a set of complex interactions designed to inspire and fold the brand more naturally into the flow as the customer designs it.

5. Sales professionals, whether direct or channel based, have always sought to be intimate with the customer. The stronger the relationship, the higher the chances are for increased sales opportunities. In reality, sales should see key moments with the customer as opportunities to enable customers with information that drives the relationship. In the Digital Helix, we refer to these opportunities as "sales as connected moments." Using the Digital Helix, the sales process is based on knowledge of the customer's inside and outside needs, interests, and desires. Nobody likes to be sold to, but everybody wants to buy. Using digital knowledge tools in near real time, Digital Helix sales interaction becomes the art of solving the problem versus simply selling.

6. In successful digital organizations, everybody is responsible for each other across the organization. The shared vision, information, and application of our internal and external interactions, as well as how we listen and come together, is vital to success and being able to outpace the competition. Without this collaboration, we miss too many powerful insights, actions, and opportunities. We call this "all for one, and one for all across the organization." This element can only work if all the components inside the organization are fluidly connected around

the themes and streams that matter. All humans want to do the right thing. The Digital Helix organization uses pathways, receptors, and rewards that empower sales to happen naturally and in near real time.

7. In the digital world, every interaction matters, and all are equally important. These interactions build on each other and offer a chance to inspire when done right or detract when missed or handled poorly. Organizations need to be able to work beyond the singular moments and make the most of each connection, while simultaneously looking and thinking about what the customer might need next. Understanding this and embracing the concept of constant regeneration is vital to building a foundation of success and achieving scale for the future. We call this "all together and one step ahead." Many great leaders argue that there are no big moments, because all moments matter. The Digital Helix organization recognizes early signs of opportunities and issues and rapidly adjusts course as needed. Digital tools for insights, collaboration, and action allow for near real-time actions. But to truly gain competitive advantage, a shift in philosophy needs to occur so that organizations can use the tools to their full potential.

The new Digital Age requires that organizations not only execute and measure their operations differently but also reevaluate how to reward behaviors and hire for certain skills. These seven components will help guide you and give you a framework to embrace the Digital Age the right way, for long-term success. Can you begin to identify how your organization would look and perform if you fully embraced the Digital Helix?

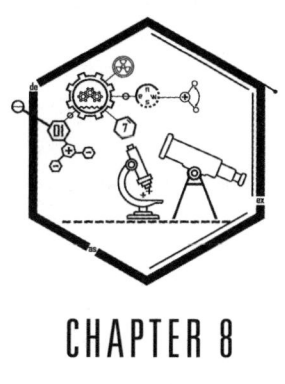

CHAPTER 8

EXECUTIVES AS DIGITAL HELIX EXPLORERS

"If things seem under control, you are just not going fast enough."
—Mario Andretti

This chapter goes into more details about what it takes to make executives true digital leaders by using the Digital Helix for success. The key idea here is to look at the underlying evidence far more critically in order to help you and the organization navigate toward being the critical drivers for digital transformation.

> "If you're not stubborn, you'll give up on experiments too soon. And if you're not flexible, you'll pound your head against the wall and you won't see a different solution to a problem you're trying to solve."[1]
>
> **—Jeff Bezos, CEO, Amazon**

To ensure the executive function delivers and helps the organization's digital transformation effort to thrive, we need to first look at two aspects that help determine success:

1. Executives need to expand their sensitivity to information and identify the most important elements in order to orchestrate the transformation in the right way. This expansion of information goes far beyond the key performance indicators most look at and requires a different set of leadership traits to shine.

2. Executives need to be increasingly capable of focusing on the potentially small and different elements that drive effective digital transformation. In digital, many times the size of an activity does not define the magnitude of its significance or capacity to make the results far greater than the sum of the parts.

What You See Is Not All There Is—Explorocracy in Practice

As mentioned, the value of any digital transformation has to far exceed the sum of all parts. Short of this goal, results are at best mixed and at worst failure. The executive's job is both proactive and guiding. Executives who sit back, review, or question results, in most cases, doom their organizations to fail. As we have seen from almost every digital transformation research study, the chance of true economic success is less than 30 percent. In business, sports, or almost any other scenario, this especially high chance of failure is unacceptable in anything but the direst situations.

Risk management is undoubtedly an inherent part of the executive's role. But when the chances are one in three against you and your organization, executives are not really managing risks. Instead, they are wagering against the odds in a rigged game. Thinking of it this way, the odds are roughly the same as having a 30 percent chance of hitting the fairway with every golf shot. Over the course of eighteen holes, you have little to no chance for sustained success. Even if at every hole you started out with a perfect shot, there would be a 70 percent chance you would miss the next two badly. Getting one or two digital projects to deliver while having the vast majority fail will never allow the effort to be worth more than the sum of its parts. In most cases, these digital transformations are actually less than the value of each part. Due to various failures and the interconnected nature of transformation, the organization winds up sliding backward. No matter the business, the executive needs to be the one driving the ship toward success and not just judging it at the end. So how do executives increase their digital transformation success rate? The secrets are a combination of noticing more and looking for what is not there.

First is the power of noticing what is happening beyond the surface level. As much as it takes precise skills to be a world-class golfer, the same is true for the Digital Helix executive. In his book, *The Power of Noticing*, Max H. Bazerman talks about elements, such as motivated blindness, whereby leaders can be distracted from looking at root challenges, true signals, or information that would enable them to make better decisions. Like a golfer might miss changing wind conditions or breaks on the green, executives often overindex on familiar metrics and miss leading indicators. These missed signs can show not only how to course correct existing digital transformations, but more importantly, where to invest in the first place. The key elements that drive executive leaders to be successful in the Digital Helix are complex, but given the overindex on data we have talked about elsewhere, being able to work outside traditional definitions of leadership is critical. Being an explorer is now more vital than ever.

> "The best leaders are 'first-class noticers.' This means they pay close attention to what is happening around them. They see things that others miss."[2]
>
> **—Max H. Bazerman, author of *The Power of Noticing***

The other key is looking for information, data, and patterns that are not readily apparent or familiar. This is how decision-making and leadership break down inside seemingly great organizations. In his book *Thinking, Fast and Slow*, which sums up his life's research on human judgments and decision-making, Daniel Kahnemen, a Nobel Prize–winning psychologist, talks about a concept called "What you see is all there is" (WYSIATI). Kahnemen explains that the benefit and curse of WYSIATI is that it allows us to make sense of partial information in a complex world. The coherent story this method generates is often close enough to reality to support reasonable action but shields us from looking deeper. Kahneman explains that WYSIATI induces a number of systemic biases, such as overconfidence and framing effects, which create fundamental flaws in human judgment.

> "The idea that the future is unpredictable is undermined every day by the ease with which the past is explained. Thus, we can be blind to the obvious, and we are also blind to our blindness."[3]
> **—Daniel Kahneman, author of *Thinking, Fast and Slow***

How does WYSIATI impact digital transformation efforts? Many times this concept prompts a tendency to accept the first thing that occurs or the first thing we see. In digital transformation, WYSIATI promotes quick decisions and entrenches the organization into a single view of what information we need or should use to make critical decisions. This view locks the organization or team into one prescribed future from the outset, often based on little information. Within your organization, how many times have you witnessed teams and executives blind or unwilling to contemplate and evaluate alternative strategic options due to the information in front of them? If we're told that certain metrics or data are all that matter, there is a high likelihood that any new digital system will either reaffirm this belief or be labeled a failure, no matter the benefit.

Executives must leverage the explorer's mindset to check natural tendencies and go well beyond the first "truths" and the surface-level familiar that is in front of them. As an executive, your key responsibility is to go far beyond what's normal and explore new paths. This exploration allows you to not only find new possibilities but also to chart the best course forward. Like a great explorer, the executive needs to explore the unusual and strive to look for information beyond where one might normally look. Digital, as we have said, changes many aspects of a business. One of these areas is decision-making. Executives who thrive in this environment are those who consistently seek more information and push teams beyond the quick and usual. This skill is key to changing the odds and successfully betting on the future of your organization.

> "We have to establish our credentials as an explorocracy; so to survive and rule ourselves, we have to explore."[4]
>
> —China Miéville, author of *Embassytown*

From our research, we found the act of comparing two similar organizations gives us a near perfect way to review the economic differences in performance between groups of organizations. This is the closest to a ceteris paribus comparison as is possible. Leaders showed incredible economic returns from everything from brand to sales, marketing, collaboration, HR-related issues, and even ROI. By comparison, lower performers with near identical designs achieved six times less economic returns.

By using an index for each of the eight variables for economic performance, we can see how radically different the outcomes look for similar profiles. Using a baseline of 100, leaders outperform others by more than eight to one in margin gain and revenue and by about five to one in market share and brand value. Remember, this is looking at similar organizations and segments or markets.

How do leaders achieve these remarkable gains? Of the 174 variables we reviewed, a number of small but critical variations illustrate the differences between an organization with a highly driven explorocracy at an executive level and one without. While some of the actions may seem similar, these small differences illustrate and in many ways amplify the magnitude of the results.

Executive Explorers Value the Journey and the Path

Executive explorers promote and push boundaries because they value the whole process of exploring. It is this appreciation for the journey and the path that causes them to invest in new forms of listening and to run extensive experiments far more often than their lower-performing peers. But it is not just the new elements and challenges that explorers value. Executive explorers crank out trainings twice as often as well. This explorer mentality shows how the best performers value and need data and information, while empowering individuals to use and leverage these resources across the organization. Additionally, explorers do not see legality and governance as constraining forces. These leaders use legality and governance as guideposts to chart their journey rather than view them as excuses for not pushing forward in certain directions.

> "CEOs either 'go with their gut' or push people to be more 'data driven.' This tends to be very crude. A more effective heuristic is when people in the organization interact with their leaders, do they feel smarter or do they feel stupider? The answers will show if the team as a whole is there to be servants to a vision or empowered by the vision to collaborate, share, and explore and experiment in different ways. Transformational leaders seek the latter and are constantly looking for the new to explore."
>
> —**Michael Schrage, research fellow at MIT Sloan School's Initiative on the Digital Economy, oversees research on digital experimentation and network effects, and is author of** *The Innovator's Hypothesis*

Executive Explorers Enable, Embrace, and then Mandate

While every organization trains its people and teams on policies, executive explorers use trainings to empower and push employees to succeed by making their own decisions based on these policies. Executive explorers help employees execute social on their own by setting clear KPIs that tie back into business objectives. In addition, explorers push to have other C-suite members actively engage in strategy and counsels with their teams to drive both thinking and integration. These factors, in combination with explorers investing more than lower-performing peers in internal platforms, show that executives set up repeatable frameworks that promote action, risk taking, and compliance with the organization's objectives.

> "Risk-taking is required to learn. To express or demonstrate what we've just learned is the risk-taking process. So environments and leaders that really value taking a shot and 'going for it' drive organizations and people to become curious and interested in what might be, as opposed to being fearful of what might not work right."
>
> **—Dr. Michael Gervais, consultant to world-class athletes and teams, cofounder, Compete To Create Consulting**

Executive Explorers Realign and Rehire as Needed

Executive explorers hire like other executives, but they are far more willing to accept and push for change and make needed shifts on the fly than their counterparts. They seek to rightly add the best skills to match their needs as they change and evolve. One way that this is achieved is through the use of external partners. Explorers add new or realign existing partners far more aggressively to get the right skills and mix for the organization. In social media, explorers are 35 percent more likely to have external vendors managing resources. These facts clearly show that these executives understand the new digital world demands and how to let go of some aspects to enable others.

> "We hire with a digital vision in mind. By embracing this digital mindset, we didn't have to retool or reskill at all, and that is what sets us apart from others that have tried to embrace digital along the way. Anytime you add new people and skills to legacy operations that are changing you are going to have significant issues with reskilling and culture change. But because we started down this digital path the right way, we were able to hire in people that had the appropriate skill set and mindset to deliver the results we expected."
>
> **—Larry Scott, commissioner, Pac-12 Conference**

Explorers Let Go and Seek More

Executive explorers understand and embrace the power of others to drive the journey, both farther and deeper. By actively engaging others, explorers find new ways to empower members of the organization to start their own explorations and journeys. If we look at social transformation, we can see explorers absolutely overindex on every facet. They are 65 percent more likely to talk about social and digital transformation with their peers and push board members and teams to actively drive wider transformation initiatives.

> "When people forcibly take control, you get an impedance mismatch, where even greater barriers are created. The best analogy is attempting to climb Mt. Everest alone without the right tools, resources, and information. There are thousands of variables that would take you a lifetime to learn in order for you to survive and thrive on your journey. You need guides, Sherpas, or catalysts to understand the goals, environment, and what is required to be successful. This broadening and widening of the team with experts in different areas makes a significant difference. This is how we develop deeper relationships while getting the best results and avoiding making costly mistakes."
>
> —Vanessa Colella, head of Citi Ventures and chief innovation officer of Citi

Becoming a Modern-Day Lewis and Clark

To become a Digital Helix executive explorer requires constant vigilance of your time, attention, language, and actions. Much of the new digital world is not mapped yet, and as brands move forward, study after study shows no more than 30 percent get digital transformation right economically. To become your organization's digital version of Lewis and Clark, you need to think about experimentation in knowledge, resource exchange, and mapping success. Exploration at its best isn't about the leader, it is about how executives enable others, empower differences, and push boundaries for themselves and others. Great executive explorers understand the power of building new and reskilled work forces and adding new dimensions in insights, and most importantly, they bring a constant energy of purpose to all aspects of digital transformation.

> "Ambition leads me not only farther than any other man has been before me, but as far as I think it possible for man to go."
> —James Cook, English explorer and cartographer, 1728–1779

Digital Requires Executives to Develop Three New Skills or Tendencies Rapidly

Exploration in the Digital Age is about the combination of three different skills beyond those that dominate traditional leadership roles. In the nondigital era, leadership tended to center on operational efficiency, better growth than competitors, and planning differentiation for long-term benefits. However, in a world of ongoing transformation, leaders must use a new compass to guide them. Through our research and experience, we have identified three key skills that help separate great digital explorers from lower performers.

Accept risk in information and enablement because it shows real ambition.

Playing it safe almost always guarantees lower performance. Accepting risk and pushing beyond comfort levels is required to deliver high performance in any situation. This understanding enables digital explorers to trust and train those for the new digital mindsets and skills that dominate startups. Fortune organizations have vast pools of capital, external partners, IT resources, and market segments. Organizations have to understand that to be successful, there is room for both risk and using old and new information to help provide the essential indicators for the digital world. The key is to identify what is best for the path and vision you have. Not all information is born of equal importance, and the ability to separate noise from signals is vital, especially as older signals become potential noises. As we have discussed, brands that consistently miss the key signals and indicators miss markets, miss opportunities, and miss their chance for the future.

Actions drive results; mandates drive inertia.

Actions vastly exceed mandates by almost ten to one in successful organizations. When we look at all the attributes of success, actions like investment and coordination from executives are ten times more economically productive than those organizations that are led by flag-waving mandates. Setting up a small project can help, but all that does is raise a flag in a place where most have neither the equity nor experience to execute. It might be far more appropriate for an executive to use Salesforce and Radian6 than focus on his or her own social presence.

The currency of new information and experimentation is vital.

Great golfers take calculated risks to win and beat the competition. Executive explorers need a similar disposition with experimentation. The key is to teach others to take calculated risks but without guaranteeing success. Explorations should motivate others to explore because the Digital Helix organization works only when all seven components interconnect and are empowered.

For executives to truly become digital explorers they need to open up their view of what is the right information for success and ensure they are not simply seeing select indicators of performance or feedback. By adding in a measure of risk taking with experimentation, executives can plot smart actions based on their organization's successes to deliver results that are far greater than the sum of their parts.

What are the steps leaders can take tomorrow to start becoming Digital Helix explorers and accelerating transformation from the top down?

Digital Transformation Tools

To get you thinking like a digital executive explorer, here are a set of questions to ask yourself to determine your leadership and organization's capacity for exploration. Think about these eight questions as they relate to your own organization so that you can understand the power of the executive leader as an explorer. True digital executive explorers can answer a definitive yes to each of the questions. In reality you or your executive leadership will have a mix of tools you already use and others that need attention for the future.

1. As the leader, are you actively looking at streams and themes of information, or are you focusing on KPI dashboards as a key management tool?
2. Are you dedicating a significant amount of time each week to becoming more digitally articulate and experimental?
3. Have you changed the way you interact and give advice in a more digital world?
4. Have you been developing new skills for you and your colleagues, as well as promoting new skills development to the wider workforce?
5. Are you pioneering new rewards systems that drive a more Digital Helix culture around you?
6. Has your language changed and adapted to be digital-centric?
7. Do you have one nagging issue that, if overcome, could help migrate the organization to more of a Digital Helix?
8. Does your organization have many examples of thinking and behaving digitally first?

Digital Transformation Perspective

What happened? The hierarchical model simply doesn't work anymore. The craftsman-apprentice model has been replaced by learning organizations, filled with knowledge workers who don't respond to top-down leadership. Seeking opportunities to lead, young people are unwilling to spend ten years waiting in line. Most important, people are searching for genuine satisfaction and meaning from their work, not just money. For example, many employees are motivated by their company's mission when it attaches itself to social and personal goals.

In response to these changes, a new generation of leaders is reshaping the best-led global companies. Authentic leaders focused on customers are replacing hierarchical leaders who focus on serving short-term shareholders. An example of this type of leader is Unilever CEO Paul Polman, who recently told the *Financial Times*, "I don't work for the shareholder. I work for consumers and my customers."[5]

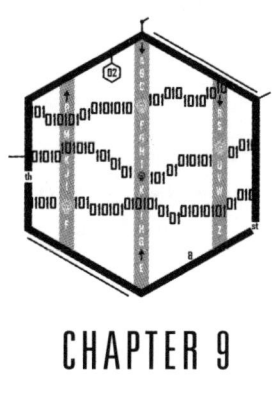

CHAPTER 9

THEMES AND STREAMS FOR INSIGHTS IN THE DIGITAL HELIX

"Distinguishing the signal from the noise requires both scientific knowledge and self-knowledge."
—Nate Silver, editor in chief, FiveThirtyEight

Remember when your children taught you how to program a VHS back in the early 1990s or set up the remote control for you? Think about five to ten years ago when your adolescent kids helped you set up your original social media accounts or showed you how to use your smartphone. Insights and ideas on how to do things in the right way don't always come from the support documents or from help files on a forum. In short, these and many more examples show how individuals are often programmed to receive and manage information. These set ways, based on how we learned to gather and parse information, can limit our ability to respond to new situations in an effective manner and create bias toward what we hear, see, learn, and do. Conversely, children can handle new and different challenges outside prescribed norms because they have the ability to focus on new and limited but incredibly powerful pieces of information without trying to fit them into preprogrammed processes.

In reality, individuals look for help and insights that tend to have immediate value or are immediately gratifying in some way. This process usually starts by using familiar sources and then filtering from there. Children, on the other hand, have remarkable capacities, often described as set shifting, that allow them to adapt to changes in the environment by switching from one mental set to another. This ability enables children to think through apparently complex challenges in simple ways and to cut through the legacy thinking and experiences that adults use to perform the same functions.

This personal or individual bias toward the familiar is also present at an organizational level. When you add this to the myopia based on urgency and delivery that exists in most organizations, you can clearly see why it is tough for organizations to think differently about the value and sources for information and decision-making. This effect and resulting bias are the conundrum that is at the heart of the theme and stream component in the Digital Helix. But overcoming this legacy sourcing and thinking is and will continue to be a critical function for successful digital transformations, since information and data are key drivers no matter the initiative or desired outcome.

> "We have moved from a fairly linear, non-real-time model where there was a lag effect between the time that we would receive feedback from our members and the time that it was synthesized and presented in a digestible format. Our new model is the 'voice of the member' model, which brings in multiple forms of member feedback and works to synthesize that feedback on a real-time basis. We have a series of tools that combine up to twenty-five different sources of member feedback across channels and touch points into a common tool. We use that tool to look for trend lines, to look for anomalies, and to do a lot of analysis and hypothesis testing around what our members are telling us and where we have issues that are systemic in nature. We use the 'voice of the member' feedback to validate what our member behavioral data tell us."
>
> **—Chris Cox, head of Digital Experience Delivery, USAA**

This chapter is designed to solve three challenges most organizations seem to suffer from when it comes to information themes (what the information is) and streams (the channels of the information that both internal and external groups use) in the digital enterprise:

1. 87 percent of organizations are investing in listening activities.
2. Most brands and groups see generally poor performance from their listening centers.
3. Only 35 percent of organizations realize a measurable net return from listening.

The paradox here is that most understand they need to listen (87 percent), but few (35 percent) can show real value from their efforts. These Fortune-type organizations are investing heavily in listening activities, usually with elaborate command centers and multitudes of data sets coming in to show they are listening. Yet for all the social and digital listening and the customer information available at an organization's fingertips, most find success and/or value is elusive. While there are any number of reasons for this, three key questions should be or should have been asked and answered to focus efforts and thus results:

1. How do we change the framework for information from architecture to delivery to extract value so that what we get delivers exponentially greater benefit than ever before?
2. What are the best practices for evolving how information is sourced and used that builds a competitive currency across every dimension of the organization from employees to partners to customers and any other body we care about?
3. What are key indicators for success or failure we should focus on as we build our theme and stream approach?

From Telescope to Living Microscope

In the pre–Digital Helix world, organizations went out searching for historical information and sources. This telescopic view most often involved collecting or even constructing findings via research and surveys. The only tricks were the illusions of finding the right representative samples of people or data and carefully looking at minimum statistically significant cells with moderate or even ridiculously low frequencies. This was, and in some cases still is, the nature of information gathering and even simulations. Sample sizes in the millions or testing and measuring hundreds of alternatives in near real-time was unfathomable due to costs and timing that would have produced findings long after the insights were needed. Digital not only changed this but also made it both feasible and cost effective to test hundreds or thousands of parameters in real time and to provide insights equally fast. In fact, brands, organizations, and even political campaigns are using this ability right now to query and test any number of variables, designs, and hypotheses they want moments after the thought pops into their heads. This living feedback can be and often is an interactive affair where brands and groups test and solicit conversations and insights from the customers and constituents they serve in real time. This is the living microscope where you can see the integrations, and it is the essence of themes and streams. Both the act of asking but also the undertaking of tapping into the places where people live online provides the rich, useful, and hyper-relevant insights needed to handle another aspect of the Digital Helix, in the moment and one step ahead.

In the digital era, sources and streams are everywhere. The real question is not about where and what to look for, but rather how do you zero in on the key nuggets that can impact your organization today and set the course for future growth?

Think of the odd contradiction we now have. Data and information is voluminous and everywhere, yet when you can find everything and track anything, what do you look for and follow? We live in a world where zettabytes of information are generated in weeks or days, if not minutes. Additionally, we can track, find, or follow how almost anything happens online via cookies and IP addresses, among others. All of this gives organizations tremendous power and a breathtakingly clear lens to tell us the exact moments that the most microscopic things happen. Think we are kidding? Read these three examples:

1. Netflix knows exactly the time you start to binge watch a show and is developing shows to meet a formula to get viewers hooked faster.
2. Grocery stores know what you are going to buy many times before you do and provide coupons to push brand choices for your next trip.
3. The New York Police Department knows where, when, and what types of crimes are most likely to be committed in the city and deploys police accordingly.

All of this shows how themes and streams are occurring and smart organizations are monitoring, analyzing, and tapping into these insights to take action. It is not that the information is completely new or organizations were completely unaware. Rather, leaders have figured out that increasing amounts of information requires increasing scrutiny of what is valuable (signal) and what is a distraction (noise). This key action enables successful organizations to move forward faster and be successful.

Digital Transformation Perspective

Using increasingly granular data, from detailed demographics and psychographics to consumers' clickstreams on the Web, businesses are starting to create highly customized offers that steer consumers to the "right" merchandise or service—at the right moment, at the right price, and on the right channel. These are called "next best offers." Consider Microsoft's success with email offers for its search engine, Bing. These emails are tailored to the recipient the moment they're opened. In two hundred milliseconds—a lag imperceptible to the recipient—advanced analytics software assembles an offer based on real-time information about him or her: data including location, age, gender, and online activity both historical and immediately preceding, along with the most recent responses of other customers. These ads have lifted conversion rates by as much as 70 percent—dramatically more than similar but uncustomized marketing efforts.

Companies often test offers through multiple channels to find the most efficient one. At CVS, ExtraCare offers are delivered through kiosks as well as on register receipts, targeted circulars, by email, and recently, via coupons sent directly to customers' mobile phones. Qdoba Mexican Grill, a quick-serve franchise, is expanding its loyalty program by delivering coupons to customers' smartphones at certain times of the day or week to increase sales and smooth demand. Late-night campaigns near universities have seen a nearly 40 percent redemption rate, whereas redemption rates average 16 percent for Qdoba's overall program. Starbucks uses at least ten online channels to deliver targeted offers, gauge customer satisfaction and reaction, develop products, and enhance brand advocacy. For example, its smartphone app allows customers to receive tailored promotions for food, drinks, and merchandise based on their SoLoMo information.

These few examples show just a bit of the incredible detail in the petri dish of living information that is available to almost any brand or group. More importantly, this vast array of knowledge and insights is growing and getting more prescriptive. While volume was historically comforting, now it can be utterly disruptive if not harnessed and parsed to provide value. This means we have to ask ourselves about what really matters in the universe of information we now have and what we should be filtering and seeking now that collecting and collating is infinitely easier than before.

The winning digital enterprise or agency needs to experiment, witness, and collaborate to find the right signals among the mass of noise we consciously, and even unconsciously, collect every moment of every day. This is the new currency for success. When information is near perfect, only the near-perfect organizations will figure out what to focus on and how to use it for a competitive advantage. These are generally skills that need to be taught, experimented with, and constantly socialized across all parts of the organization, as certain streams could have incredibly valuable insights at key moments.

All of this shows that information is a constant flow. In the Digital Helix, the act of listening is not enough. You need to listen with intent and screen far more than you pick up. The secret is understanding the three variables that drive success:

1. How you collect information may be more important than what you collect and requires constant examination.
2. What constitutes value for pieces of information and how combinations of data and sources can be used to deliver even greater value.
3. How you decide to deliver and adjust information becomes vital.

"We only succeed if our customers succeed. That's why their insights and feedback are invaluable to how we innovate at speed and scale."
—**Karen Mangia, vice president, Customer Insights, Salesforce**

A whole new science of applied information is just around the corner. The parlor trick with information in the Digital Helix organization is a set of sequenced steps that allow you to amplify, glue, ignore, or enable new information to come in and then maybe out of the framework. It is these themes and streams that then become the focus for listening. The following questions are ones you should ask yourself and your teams frequently to increase the value of information for your organization. Clearly, we would like you to be able to say yes emphatically to each of these. However, we know that there are different states of awareness and maturity. The best organizations we have worked with or interviewed show strong performance across each of these seven areas:

1. Are you sharing cross-functional and departmental streams of information far more often than ever before?

   "Our company is organized with the idea that we need to manage our enterprise information distribution strategy at an experience level. By structuring ourselves this way we are able to better identify what we need to do to be successful as well as work across functions and channels to better meet our members' needs within a digital framework."
   —**Chris Cox, head of Digital Experience Delivery, USAA**

2. Can you quickly adjust information needs as you see behaviors and opportunities change?

   "In 2000, Hallmark came to the realization that greeting cards alone would not allow us to achieve our growth objectives. This realization led to a shift in strategy to complement the greeting card business with other forms of growth through innovation.

We knew we could use the enormous trust in the Hallmark brand to our advantage if we had the right information at the right time and could leverage it to shift our overall strategy quickly with our customers' new needs in mind."
—**Lisa Macpherson, CMO/SVP marketing, Hallmark**

3. Are all levels of the organization sharing ideas about themes for information?

    "How would a better understanding of the people you're trying to serve, internally or externally—understanding them, empathizing with them—how would that help you make better decisions and better execute on your strategy? Listening to them, sharing stories with them, and engaging with them—those are my three pillars of visual approximation and visual leadership. Can you listen, share, and engage?"
    —**Charlene Li, principal analyst, Altimeter, a Prophet company**

4. How have you changed the way you interact with information to act faster?

    "Technologies like IBM's Watson are able to ingest both structured and unstructured data. This is incredibly powerful because unstructured data is the language of humanity. By understanding this data we're able to understand people as individuals with deeper and deeper levels of detail. This level of understanding is going to be increasingly relevant in the future. We must ask our customers, 'How much more can we learn about you, and therefore, how much more relevant can we be as we serve you?'"
    —**Jon Iwata, senior vice president, marketing and communications, IBM**

5. Is the organization developing new skills to handle information differently?

"A lot of people come from Silicon Valley with in-depth tech knowledge and knowledge of agile methods and DevOps, which is good, but they don't necessarily have the same appreciation for the fact that the value in becoming truly digital comes from transforming how the work is done and the skills that are needed to be successful. Creating digital value across an organization means you must have the patience to dive into the existing processes and say, 'Is this process still necessary? If not, can we get rid of it? If it is still necessary, how can we make it faster, better, more efficient, whatever the case might be?' This type of mindset requires a transformational skill set."
—**David Bray, CIO, Federal Communications Commission**

6. Are there new rewards that have been instituted to drive a more Digital Helix culture around you in terms of information (gathering, dissemination, and analysis)?

"In the IT world with the kind of rapid change and complexity of what we do, it's less effective to try to micromanage or command and control the people who are doing the work. You're hiring people with technical skills that hopefully go beyond your skills, so you can't really tell them what to do, in a sense, because they know better than you. What you need to be doing at the management level is setting the vision, the target, setting up incentives that encourage people to move in the right directions, finding ways to communicate what the agency or the organization is trying to do, and then molding the behavior of those people."
—**Mark Schwartz, chief information officer, US Citizenship and Immigration Services**

7. Is there a revised process to get new information into your current management themes and streams?

> "We often talk about how we constantly need new skills and new ways of working to be most effective. The 'old school' thinking is that leaders know and have the right answers. To be successful today, we have to combine this thinking with curiosity and openness to the idea of leaders not having all the answers and being willing and able to set the example of asking more questions. If we are not asking the questions, we are not finding the solutions."
>
> —**Vanessa Colella, head of Citi Ventures and chief innovation officer of Citi**

As discussed, it is often easy to look at the volume of information and the vast array of sources it comes from in the digital enterprise as a soothing sign of being in control. It is easy to believe that among all these sources and all these pieces of information you will be able to find valuable truths to guide the organization to the next level. In fact, this is the illusion of control and the opposite of what it takes to make information valuable. To create real value requires not just access to the information but extraordinarily good filtering and contextual skills across teams and the organization. Team members as well as senior management, in both their daily leadership styles and line management, need to be comfortable with this change of lens.

Leaders in the old world argued that information was power. In truth, information is infinitely available, and therefore the knowledge about how to use it is the vital ingredient for success. Now, information not only tells us what a customer did or liked, it informs business models and instant business decisions. This is where themes and streams meet the sales moments and marketing communications that matter. But in order to do any of this, businesses that use data to drive daily or hourly decisions have to understand the needs of the consumer, provide information and value to the consumer at the moments that matter, and alter the business to accommodate all of this to positively impact the business. Without getting the right data at the right time, businesses cannot ensure that they have the products, features, or services needed to impact sales. In addition, consumers have to understand the value above and beyond the competition, so this information also has to be delivered in the times and places where the consumer wants it. This information dance requires an active themes and streams engine with adequate levers within the business to adjust (otherwise the insights are for naught).

Think about Uber and its business model. While Uber's streams seem commonplace to us, they were unheard of just a little while ago. The Uber model uses everyday business information streams complemented with geolocation, click behavior, social data, online commentary, search information, and algorithms that add one piece of data to another to create exponentially more value. What is more, there are hundreds of smaller examples within every organization, but most are used in small teams or isolation.

Once you recognize the power of these themes and streams, filtering becomes the vital skill. Success comes from not only the information placed in front of you but also the understanding of the themes and the streams as well as the moment they are being delivered. The trick is to go back to something we said in the first chapter: "To succeed, leaders need to make sure all their digital investments work together and deliver value that is measurable and greater than the sum of their parts." This mantra is especially true for each component, and doubly so for themes and streams. Successful digitally transformed organizations all exhibit a more confident view of the future than many of those that are struggling in the process. Confidence in our own futures will be dominated by our ability to be flexible, be responsive, and learn how to filter in relevant and filter out potentially irrelevant but highly available information for decision-making.

Thinking about listening more in the guise of the themes and streams of information is critical in the Digital Helix. Take this example from the former vice president of marketing at Hallmark brands, Lisa Macpherson. Hallmark is an archetypal American retail brand, but the advent of digital delivery and the enormous value of socially sharing emotions in near real time for free created immense pressure to change in order to find the right feedback from the right channels at the right moments to maximize value.

> "We had metrics and business processes that focused on assessing marketing campaigns after the campaign was over. We would do exhaustive analysis of all the various measures and objectives set up for a campaign and think about how we would do it differently the next time. With the advent of digital marketing, the ability

to microtarget, the ability to be in multiple channels at once, we needed to set much more granular measures, things that were more predictive of the ultimate sales results, whether they were click-throughs or eyeballs or actions taken. We were able to look at much more granular measures, look at them much more frequently, and then develop the business processes and culture to evolve and learn and experiment much more quickly, and to do so while the campaign was still active. That meant that we could optimize the marketing effort in flight and very real time, and not wait for the next season or the next campaign or the next new product to use those learnings. So it was a very systematic change in how we set objectives, how we set measures and metrics, how we tracked those, how we acted on those, and then, culturally, being willing to work with a little less data and more hypotheses on what to do differently while the campaign was still in flight."

—Lisa Macpherson, CMO/SVP of marketing, Hallmark

When you have these themes and streams coming together, you get a real and actionable picture of the situation in real time. The process of listening, filtering, and ultimately combining relevant data to identify and make the right moves in an instant is what theme and stream allow. Asking the right questions and getting the organization set up to handle the process before jumping into action is what separates the leaders from the laggards. Can you identify signals and noise in your organization that would bring you closer to using a themes and streams approach?

CHAPTER 10

CUSTOMERS HAVE EXPERIENTIAL PORTFOLIOS

"Knowledge speaks, but wisdom listens."
—Jimi Hendrix

It sounds like common sense that consumers, business buyers, or even citizens in the Digital Age are building a portfolio of experiences every time they engage a brand or agency. In fact, most marketers are so in tune with this that billions of dollars annually are spent on providing, refining, and drawing people in to the experience. But this is a one-sided view. Yes, your organization can and should provide the best experience for your customers or users. But have you thought about the inverse from the customer's perspective?

Every time a product is purchased, a service is delivered, or a friend talks about how to best use the product or what to avoid, the portfolio is being built. While to you or even to the customer themselves this may seem like a series of slightly isolated elements, they do collide at some point. This is how people handle and filter the massive amounts of information thrown at them from every corner of their physical and virtual world. For example, you could be shopping with a friend who bought a product and mentioned they did not like it. In the digital world, this could be reviews or ratings presented as you shop. It can all happen in a few seconds because of the technologies consumers, citizens, and business influencers have at their fingertips. This radically shifts the power base in good and bad ways and directly onto the backs of the people you are trying to reach and convince.

> "Digital makes the hard easy. It makes esoteric commonplace. But most of all, it makes things that used to be fairly time consuming real time."
>
> **—Michael Schrage, research fellow at MIT Sloan School's Initiative on the Digital Economy, oversees research on digital experimentation and network effects, and is author of** *The Innovator's Hypothesis*

You can think of it like a financial portfolio, where all the parts are connected. In the worst case, your organization is vulnerable if it does not handle one of the pieces of the portfolio well enough. All of the good you do as an organization can be dismissed if a key piece of the portfolio does not deliver. Take, for example, great product reviews. Earning a "five-star" rating at the purchase phase is not enough if you have troublesome service and support, since all pieces of the journey are now connected. A bad experience in one phase can drive overall ratings and portfolios down. Amazon or Cars.com, along with thousands of other sites, show you how reviews and the specific details of your portfolio are presented and scored instantly for would-be buyers. In fact, 90 percent of Yelp users say that positive reviews affect their buying choices,[1] and 93 percent of people who conduct research on review sites typically make purchases at the businesses for which they search.[2] But the key here is that this is not done in isolation, and a review or comment across any item in your portfolio is all that is needed to carry favor for your product or service vs. another. Look at it in the positive: A well-balanced portfolio where everything is delivering can add enormous value simply through the act of being connected. In addition, buyers leverage their portfolio with making brand choices to specify the consideration set of features, benefits, and must-haves for products and services they want. All of this points to why brands that have more "connected" positives tend to have greater market velocity for their products or services.

The key is to deliver the best experience across each phase and touchpoint, from reviews to search to pricing to service to support and ultimately to feedback. This seems obvious, right? Deliver across the board and you win. But the portfolio shifts and compresses over time while still being interconnected. As new information is delivered constantly and instantly and the buyers' needs shift, their portfolio of experience morphs as well. This radically changes the overall impact of negatives or positives with the brand and its competitors. That is why understanding customers' or citizens' complete experiential portfolios is vital.

> "There will be different ways for consumers to access content. So, everyone needs to be a lot more flexible in working with and understanding their consumers. For us at the Pac-12, we have already begun thinking about tailoring our offerings to give fans more of what they want in the format that they want it in. We are already planning on how to use and find more information and data about our fans from existing and new sources. This is and will be the backbone of engaging and connecting with our fans across both digital/social media as well as working closely with our schools through various initiatives to drive fan engagement to new levels. Using more tailored and targeted efforts driven by our understanding of what our fans value is core to providing the best experience and continually improving it."
> —**Larry Scott, commissioner, Pac-12 Conference**

Identifying and handling the interconnected experiences within the portfolio is where most organizations fail and exactly where digital is supposed to help the most. Many times the isolated systems and groups responsible for tracking and monitoring these feedback loops are to blame. ERP, CRM, social feedback, customer support, competitive pricing reviews, communications, and sales feedback have to connect based off the near real-time information an organization can access. These pain points need to be identified and adjusted to make yours a winning portfolio.

In our experience in this area with brands both big and small, there tends to be a wide gap between organizations that are digitally transformed and those that are not. Digital leaders have built their portfolios and connected insights to allow the buyer to self-navigate. Laggards, on the other hand, know the theory for connecting insights but have not correctly invested leveraging and surfacing these insights in a connected manner. From our research, we have found that the most transformed enterprises didn't do only one form of social engagement with customers; they invested in a huge range of activities. From crowdsourcing new product ideas to service and support to demand generation and even stockholder engagement through social, the underlying philosophy was to connect all these elements. These leading organizations did so through various departments or functions with the goal of building their set of experiences and inputs into a complete portfolio across all facets of the brand.

The Catherine wheel in figure 10.1 offers potential elements that contribute to any organization's portfolio of experiences. This diagram covers the full range of elements, including products/services (experiences), the company overall, and even the nature of the customer's sales and marketing interactions (moments). Now, these all compress either in parallel or at least in pairs (peer and market feedback, for example) and nearly always in real time.

Customer power is the new driving force, and an organization's ability to respond, interact, and comanage becomes the key indicator of successful digital transformation. This highlights the vital nature of the connections inside the DNA of your digital organization. Take a look inside each strand of the Digital Helix. Each shows us the forms of digital behaviors and processes that are necessary for success. Following are some examples.

In chapter 8, on executives as digital explorers, we discussed the essential behaviors, attitudes, and actions that would drive successful digital transformations from the top. We have seen ideas around the concept of "customer first" work well here when executives have the full picture and understanding of their customers' portfolios. Successful executives choose the key customer portfolio moments and drive focus and knowledge of each throughout the organization. Leaders use this information live to deliver personalized experiences. They understand how instant and customized can amplify the needs of each component in the portfolio to highlight the right focus for the customer and deliver meaningful change in ROI. Furthermore, we have also seen mistakes made when leaders try to build a complex model to attack portfolios as a kick-off point. It is far too tough for even the most mature and traditional organizations to absorb significant changes without digital processes and DNA to act on the findings or recommendations.

Figure 10.1: Customers' Portfolio of Experiences

A model naturally follows as organizations absorb and set up the digital DNA to handle the shift to portfolios based on the insights and dynamics faced. But the model only comes about and works after vast improvements in collective awareness of the portfolio itself as well as of the areas that require attention. From there, the teams must be set up to handle collaborative resolutions regardless of the goal or issue. As mentioned, a highly digitally transformed organization can perform faster than their less digital counterparts in this regard. For example, we have twice seen the results in developing and implementing programmatic designs in social engagement when architected right. Here is where the relevant role of the executive as a digital explorer shows its value. Executives who focus the organization around maximizing the value of the customer portfolio know this to be true. By bringing resources to bear for the key aspects of the portfolio (through both small and tangible examples), executives rally the organization around key issues to solve and grow.

Looking at the theme and stream component is also vital for resolving or leveraging customer portfolio components. Customer satisfaction surveys and Net Promoter Scores tend to give color to customers' views of the business and offerings. However, these do not identify the key portfolio elements that are critical to an organization's long-term success.

Digital leaders need to think about how to identify and incorporate new customer themes into their marketing and customer satisfaction equations to improve the portfolio offerings. For example, seeing a product get only neutral feedback at launch or little to no positive customer service feedback is a leading indicator in the new digital world. In addition, information themes may well come via streams such as letters or calls to executives. In addition to these examples, digital leaders have the ability to use all of the components of their digital DNA to recognize, properly evaluate, and drive the right course of action to truly make positive impacts on the customer's portfolio.

> "The banking business is very mature, and Citi has been around for over 200 years. Even as an established player, we cannot assume that we know our customers' pain points. We push to validate, even if we think we have a potential solution for their needs. We challenge each other to solve these pain points by learning, testing, and validating to understand the best ways to roll out these solutions efficiently and effectively. Our systematic model has created an environment where making changes is faster and more plausible than it has ever been before. For large established financial institutions, we are spending a lot of time trying to understand not only how we make use of technologies to make our existing processes more efficient and deliver to

customers ever-better products and services, but the right way to step into this completely different kind of world where people and customers are attempting to reimagine the industry before someone else does first."

—**Vanessa Colella, head of Citi Ventures and chief innovation officer of Citi**

Sales as connected moments, by definition, will only function with a full understanding of the customer's complete portfolio of experiences that might affect the sales processes and outcomes. Imagine knowing all the experiences a customer has with the brand and potentially with your competition. Now, think about your sales process and how it would benefit from:

1. Better access to the right people with the right portfolio and offering
2. The ability to target key sales moments
3. Being able to show higher value for your offering, including more repeat value or a lower cost of acquisition

The stronger the understanding and management of customer portfolios inside your organization, the more effective sales moments can be to deliver beyond current scope or competitor offerings. This may sound a little far-fetched, but this level of vision into the minds and experiences of the customer is a huge advantage for the company. Knowing the value placed by the customer as well as the value the customer assigns to you and your competitors gives you the complete customer experiential portfolio to use across the entirety of the funnel. When we have helped organizations migrate from a traditional to the moments-based sales model, we have seen them leverage this knowledge and vastly expand their targeting, selling, and closing capabilities. But to rise to this level requires the ability to share portfolio information in near real time with a team able to access and leverage it.

Marketing and communications as a flow offers an important layer to the customer's experiential portfolio because it can deliver a coordinated set of actions through key parts of the customer's experiences that matter in pre-, during, and post-purchase moments. As with sales, for connected moments, having the ability to identify and use your customer's portfolio to your optimal advantage, while also using it to depose your competitors, is a significant benefit. Portfolio strength can identify marketing and communication strategies and tactics that lay the groundwork for sales and help differentiate your offering. In addition, knowing the customer's portfolio and values enables organizations to drive and promote buying criteria that favors your brand.

A great example of this as well as product development is between Apple and Android. Both have similar smartphone offerings in terms of capabilities, features, and benefits. Yet most iPhones sell for twice what their Android competitors sell for. A key reason for this is the value placed on experience. Apple's marketing of their experience and "ease of use" is born out of the knowledge of its customer's portfolio and perceived value for technology that "just works." The company exploits this experience to drive pricing premiums across phones as well as their other products while helping set buying criteria for the market. While not 100 percent foolproof, having twice the pricing advantage and forcing competitors to react to your criteria has had huge advantages dating back to the original Macintosh computers. With digital transformation and the knowledge and insights they have gained, Apple has been able to accelerate this advantage over formidable competitors like Google and Samsung.

> "You have got to start with the customer experience and work backwards to the technology."
> —**Steve Jobs, founder and former CEO, Apple**

Because your customer's portfolio of experiences covers such a wide array, it is essential and almost a prerequisite that everybody has to be responsible to everybody else. In almost every case, there is not a single point or group that has the scope to turn numerous insights into portfolio results. Managing and leveraging the potential power of your customer's portfolio of experiences requires digital technologies that enable cross-platform sharing and curation of insights via many forms, including internal to external social, instant messaging, and collaboration as a backbone for success.

Precisely this agility and long-range thinking, combined with the responsibility to each other and provided by the right tools, can set up an organization to drive portfolio success or seal its fate.

Organizations designed around the customer's portfolio of experiences are, by definition, in the moment and one step ahead. As an organization, these digital leaders are capable of understanding the blips, trends, and quick shifts that can change the velocity and shape of the market as well as their customer's portfolios. Understanding and using this one-step-ahead philosophy matters because it is a constantly evolving process. Digital leaders use tools and processes to identify and harness these evolutions. Further, these organizations accept that constant change can be utilized to drive real growth when the whole of the company is aligned to leverage the customer's experiential portfolio. This, too, requires a balance. Too much focus on customer service feedback or competitive feedback can distort the priorities of the organization and cloud the real values inside the portfolio. This can lead to being in the moment but not being truly one step ahead, as organizations tend to miss new moments when overindexing on existing ones. This fact alone is an illustration of how important it is to be consistently one step ahead and to keep everything connected to the customer's portfolio of experiences.

> "In health care, we need to remember that we are not competing just with the hospital system across town. We're competing with the experiences that our patients have with Amazon and Google, with how easy it is to find something, order it, and have it delivered with just a click or two. And now, it's not just Amazon who delivers that experience. All kinds of businesses are moving fast to change their customer experience. Customers now expect every industry to keep up with that level of experience. It is our job to identify and meet the experiences customers want now and anticipate the experiences they will want in the future."
> —**Kelly Faley, vice president, digital marketing, Sharp HealthCare**

Unfortunately, there isn't a complete model to measure the full value or effect of the customer portfolio on the value of a company's economic value or equity like Interbrand's Best Global Brands Report. Leading digital organizations understand and have identified the components that drive that customer portfolio equity like some of the elements we have discussed (increases selling price, faster time to close sales, shorter sales cycles, etc.). In addition, these leaders used the metrics they had to validate the benefits without waiting for a market-ready performance index to prove them right. The best organizations have worked diligently to leverage each of the other DNA components to drive exceptional value in their customer's portfolio and have used metrics in place today to identify and change as needed. They have also gone one step further and recognized the need to bring each of these digital DNA components into play together to complement each other.

Make no mistake, there are significant challenges to getting all the other six DNA components working together to improve your portfolio value in the eyes of your customers. Even with Net Promoter scores, customer satisfaction indexes, and all the data that comes with them, vaunted brands like Toyota and Lexus have had to reorganize and reevaluate how best to structure themselves to make and leverage the shift. But in the case of the winners, they have used these challenges as opportunities to set themselves up for the next round and to stay ahead.

The DNA of the most successful digitally transformed organizations is less about grandiose statements or mandates and far more about the careful orchestration of knowledge sharing, collaboration, processes, and a constant vigilance to look for small but important shifts in dynamics. As we have mentioned, the role of the senior executive is vital here. But so, too, are others across the organization. Digital requires tools and technology, but it always runs on the strength of its people and teams. Our research shows that an unusually high focus on distributed ownership and collective measurements drives success. That pattern alone should be your first sign about how to move toward a customer experiential portfolio as one of the seven digital components of the digitally transformed enterprise.

If the present is about increasingly putting the customer first, then we must do so in their combined experiences, not only in purchasing or service. We cannot continue to think of our actions solely along "how do we serve customers better." They need to evolve and involve a major shift in how we collectively share responsibilities in a digital-centric world where the whole range of ongoing customer experiences drive purchasing decisions.

Can you see how your organization's portfolio is perceived and how it compares to that of competitors?

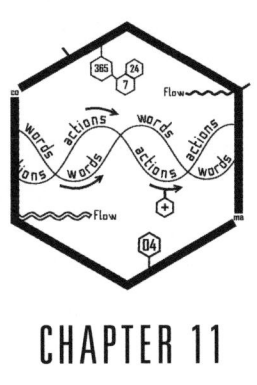

CHAPTER 11

MARKETING AND COMMUNICATIONS AS A FLOW

"Life is a series of natural and spontaneous changes. Don't resist them; that only creates sorrow. Let reality be reality. Let things flow naturally forward in whatever way they like."
—Lao Tzu

Throughout the history of marketing and certainly for most marketers' careers, almost every form of marketing or communications has been planned and managed by quarterly and/or annual goals and reviews. Marketing plans, product launches, crisis management readiness, loyalty programs, and all forms of commutations (stock holder, employee, PR, etc.) have been tied to this rhythm. And, many times, these activities have also been done in semi-glorious isolation from each other. The reason for this is that management usually needs its teams to deliver against specific targets and goals and report results back every few months. Even if your organization is more dynamic, chances are your budgeting process forces you into this regular timing and cadence.

> "The value of middle management is in driving focus. If you were to eliminate them, it would create a control and focus gap in the company."
> **—John Steinert, chief marketing officer, TechTarget**

It was then management's job to make sure things worked together and that these results boiled up to the greater goals. If things were working, you could ask/beg for more money and resources to do more or shift direction based on your results. But customers and competition don't always work within your cycles. How many of us have been pushed to drop everything because of a new "idea" from senior leaders? Add in the pressure to do more with less, and you can see why this dilemma has been ongoing long before digital arrived. So, like most of us, you probably walked this tightrope trying to balance quarterly goals and budgets with competitive and customer pressures while adjusting to the digital realities of instant information and unlimited experimentation. If you happened to be successful, it was in spite of this tug-of-war process. If you ever failed, it could well be because you did not balance your efforts between the traditional and the digital.

Digital gives us a chance to know the customer better, a lot better. This is true about what they want, but more importantly about how they act, think, and get information. Customer knowledge is critical, and most organizations do a pretty good job of surveying customers and watching their behavior. But where does this activity take place, what information is collected, and who gets the data and when? In most companies or teams, it is the marketing department. If there is sharing of the information (like the corporate and marketing planning initiatives), it will likely be done in glorious isolation. Even if you are one of the rare organizations that live off data and spread it across the company, chances are you are still planning in cycles. In either case, you are working from inside the organization out to the customer and not starting with the customer. There is a better way to deliver for your customers and deal with competition. And there is also a way to increase value and speed where digital, instead of being a piece of the puzzle, becomes a connecting thread that brings everything together.

> "We're trying to make it easy for our members to engage with us initially digitally and then moving on from there depending on their individual needs. We want to deliver an absolutely world-class experience for our members by being digitally focused but not digital only."
>
> **—Chris Cox, head of Digital Experience Delivery, USAA**

One route many have tried is investing heavily in technologies that deliver near real-time information sharing and collaboration. The theory of this approach is that the more we share and the more we collaborate, the better the decisions will be. Sharing of customer information and knowledge can certainly be increased via this route. Other marketing leaders have looked to force a comingling of people, teams, skills, and/or knowledge across functions, hoping to bring consensus and better ideas to the overall group. In either case, digital plays a vital role. Whether it is a foundational element like Salesforce, Marketo, or other cross-organizational tools or individual solutions like WebEx and SharePoint, more technologies are being implemented to increase real-time information sharing. When done right, either approach will make the company more knowledgeable on many fronts. But the act of simply buying and using software or technology does not automatically deliver a more effective organization that excels at working together. Also, while both technologies have their merits and are capable of producing results, they suffer from the same issues. Each tries to use forced collaboration as a crutch for the balancing act we all do between planning cycles, customer knowledge, and cross-group sharing.

> "We're definitely collaborating much more because it's risky not to do so, especially in a highly regulated environment. Too many things can and will go wrong if companies aren't collaborating and working together."
> **—Jeff Winton, senior vice president of corporate affairs and chief communications officer at Astellas Pharma**

The missing piece is the rhythm or flow of the customers and our market. Organizational timing and collaboration aside, being better connected and having a better understanding of others in the group or company does not inherently solve the rhythm and flow of our markets, customers, and competition. The fundamental philosophies driving more collaboration, greater skills, and shared knowledge are still based on a brand's outward view of the world. Customers are often reduced, even in customer-centric organizations, to targets that are not necessarily equal or even greater in the mix.

Again, this in many ways is similar to the ways people tried to adapt sailing ships to the steam revolution by adding engines to the old hulls. Now, like then, you can't just add technology (either organizationally and/or at an individual level) and expect the results to change by magnitudes. The addition of the technology itself adds new challenges and issues. For ships, the hulls were not made for the additional weight of the engines and fuel, therefore many failed rather dynamically. For marketing and communications, the additional digital infrastructure has created more information to parse, and in many cases, information overload can hinder efforts to be efficient. We are at a point where most organizations are using the digital data smartly, albeit in the old time-based paradigm. How do we break this mold and get better results that can be sustained and drive our momentum?

First we have to recognize the world, the market, and the premise that brings us to this point. Bringing teams together to share in their processes and giving them more data is not enough when consumers can instantly switch between all the possible marketing and communications activities from yours and every other brand instantly. From search to social to peer feedback to product reviews to email, information is available to anyone instantly. And this movement can occur anytime in really any way (digital or offline), 24/7, and certainly 365 days a year across the globe. This means the customers and their actions have evolved well beyond the traditional, but most of our functions have just added digital elements to traditional marketing and communications. As marketers, should we not try to channel the customer's momentum the way a judo master does when flipping a bigger opponent, rather than trying to reshape it to our internal processes and traditional approaches?

> "So what we're seeing today is that companies that are new-market creators are not just creating 'new markets' in the digital domain but are colliding with traditional industries. Whether you're running an international hotel chain or a regional taxi service, you're starting to see companies that are making use of technology to reimagine what industries will look like."
>
> —**Vanessa Colella, head of Citi Ventures and chief innovation officer, Citi**

We need to think differently about how to structure the way we work together to deliver without disrupting the customer's flows in the process. Customers see all forms of marketing and communications as part of one flow in their real-time worldview. This means we need to adjust the way we work, think, interact, and plan around the idea of the customer's flow. Also, one function (yes, including marketing) cannot solve the challenge or grasp the whole opportunity in the customer's view and moments. There are too many variables and combinations that exist for one function to be successful. The customer touches sales, support, and accounting, to name a few. Therefore, we need to flow our efforts and interactions to match the customer's across both direct and indirect customer interactions.

To be successful, organizations with winning digital DNA approaches use marketing and communications as a flow focused on four key behaviors that drive more success:

1. Information is seen less as a proof point and more as an ongoing way to adjust dynamically.

The constant noise makes it difficult in a digital environment to filter useful from interesting or distracting information. This challenge is heightened by the group or purpose of marketing (focusing on demand vs. brand or communications, for example). What might be considered positive information in one aspect of the equation may have little to no immediate impact on another aspect. This means critical data may be missed or shelved. A perfect example of this is when customer social questions show a need and marketing promotes a solution that solves their problem. Sales would also help the process to create demand with pricing or offers, and everything is backed up by support helping to guide use. The equation comes full circle as customers share, post, and discuss the answer/product across off- and online channels, thus expanding the flow to others (both new and current customers). In this example, data is used to adjust the interactions with the flow and guide response and actions, as well as promote success.

2. Marketing is used as an immediate and bidirectional channel.

In a world where breaking through with your message requires extraordinary effort, marketing must be vigilant in order to communicate today, and to know where to act in the future. For example, typical communications and messaging can break through and be seen in social, tracking research, media analysis, etc. In demand marketing, the breakthrough is often seen in response rates, sales feedback, win/loss, or channel feedback. In the digital world, these all collide far faster and closer than ever before, which empowers smart organizations to use feedback to drive faster adjustments. The more an organization's functions connect, share, and make rapid small or even larger adjustments, the better. Part of what drives success for marketing and communications as a flow in the digitally transformed organization is the sense of shared responsibility and ownership around everything—not just the defined areas of personal or group responsibility. This helps drive rapid and effective reactions to market changes that are more common than ever before.

3. Customer preference wins over all other competing demands.

Everything we have discussed in the previous two points you should be able to clearly see. Where marketing and communications go off the rails is when competing priorities and fiefdoms come into play. When two or more people or groups have different ideas, who wins? In most organizations, it is either the stronger or the higher-ranked group or leader. But this is not always best or preferred by the customers. That is the ultimate acid test, and it can only be answered with data, not feelings. If your organization is looking at your customers' flows, most answers are straightforward. When the answers are not straightforward, the data and experimentation provide the right course of action. If marketing and communications do not have this driving philosophy or principle, any action(s) might serve the purpose of one of the groups or initiatives but not be in alignment with the experience that best benefits the customer. Given the connected nature of customers' information flows across social to sales to messaging to content, the need to connect actions together on one guiding principle and in one flow is vital. Now, nothing occurs in isolation for a customer. In order for an organization to act quickly and effectively, these functions need to be given strong guiding principles that add focus versus trying to do everything at once and being too slow or too fragmented. This is also true in almost every case but especially where organizations need to make the best choice from a few suboptimal options. In these cases, where the best solution is not ready or available, having a flow mentality can help you choose the best option as an organization in almost an instant. But, throughout the flow, this mentality can also help guide the communication and ensure support of this lesser of two evils. This is seen as the organization uses its digital tools and data to inform and support today's reality with tomorrow's new solution.

4. Planning is a series of tests and experiments backed by data.

As we discussed, internal timing is nothing that should be used to change or manage the flow of the customer. Rather, your customer's flow should dictate your time and planning. The best way to do this is to budget for tests and experiments, while putting capital behind the best options and continuing to test and experiment. In practice, this is not much different from the process today. The biggest change is that every big plan or idea has a testing phase before the full effort. Some will say that this is not always possible with tight timelines or launches where you have to start big right away. But if you are living with and in your customers' flows, you should be able to understand what they want. This gives you the ability to pretest using your digital tools and to use the best options when a testing phase is not possible. This should give you a pretty good answer with or without a lead time. Also, the fact that customers choose what information they get and where they get it means that anything you do must be coordinated across the customers' experiential portfolios. Your efforts need testing on the external side to see what works but also on the internal side to ensure idea, form, and function work near perfectly.

By now you should be able to see that the key to better customer understanding is mapped to setting up and working within the customer's dynamic rhythm while using a constant flow of in-the-moment information, all backed by continual testing and experiments. This gives every group a chance to deliver better for the customer because the group now better knows what is needed, and they are prepared to operate in the same dynamic fashion and rhythm as the customer.

This effort is tied to the other Digital Helix components. Organizations need to share information to get the customer moments right (theme and streams) or the flow may be missed. In addition, shift planning and cycles require leading by example (executive explorer). Changes cannot occur if the leader does not fully understand and walk in the customers' footsteps to experience the world the way they see it. This is especially true in the marketing and communications areas where intensity of planning, decreasing human resources, and a vast increase in data or intelligence does not guarantee a more outward-centric approach. Marketing truly delivers with a better understanding of the customer and a shared perspective of the connected parts of the organization coming together.

> "We have a common framework through which we pipe a lot of the member feedback in a process. We combine member feedback across channels and touch points into a common tool, and we use that tool to look for trend lines and anomalies and to do a lot of analysis and hypothesis testing. This ensures that we've included the voice of our members to drive our prioritization efforts."
> **—Chris Cox, head of Digital Experience Delivery, USAA**

Those organizations with better connections throughout are 89 percent more likely to have a competitive edge over their competition, and 87 percent show better signs for growth. If the very act of managing communications and marketing as a flow around those target moments or journeys can bring far greater success, then we need to focus on this new direction for design and execution being a priority. The digital world moves too fast to try and guess or judge it each time. Constant information from multiple streams means we need a vital bond between marketing and communications more than ever before.

Kristin Lamoureux, associate dean at New York University's Tisch Center for Hospitality and Tourism, noticed in her research that "Millennials need to have experiences that are meaningful. They want to get closer to the natural environment, to the social environment, and they want to have an authentic experience."[1] Think about your products or services in this context. How can you deliver an "authentic experience" without being in the flow and free to experiment? Millennials and other generations are now being trained to look and expect an "authentic experience" from every brand. This is their definition, not yours, but your organization has to live up to it. This "authentic experience" has to flow across all touchpoints and groups within the organization with which they interact, every time. Digitally transformed winners are changing their mindset and using the tools they have to clearly understand how this seemingly small change in perspective from inside out to flow can dramatically shift efficacy, results, and experience to really deliver for your customers now and in the future.

How many customers have you directly talked to during the last week, and how many should you be talking to every month going forward to better understand and deliver?

CHAPTER 12

SALES ARE CONNECTED MOMENTS

"It seems essential, in relationships and all tasks, that we concentrate only on what is most significant and important."
—Søren Kierkegaard

Relationships matter. Successful relationships are two-way and ongoing dialogues that deliver lasting benefits for all parties. These relationships rely on a combination of listening and interacting so each party can respond to actions, languages, and ideas even when they may be out of the norm. This type of communication produces a fundamental confidence and mindset so that even when unknown variables enter, there is enough history and experience that the relationship will survive and may even prosper. This process is tested, day in and day out, and has endured for centuries or more. You can look at your own successful relationships and see where mutually understood meanings of critical moments help drive trust and push a relationship deeper.

These fundamental facts or truths about relationships do not change in the context of sales or customer relationships. Trust and confidence are the ingredients needed to create a meaningful and long-lasting B2C or B2B. We must trust that the retailer can deliver what we want and is able and willing to handle our issues promptly and effectively. At a more profound level, businesses should be able to direct and guide customers, whether brick and mortar stores or in a B2B setting, to the best solution for their needs at any given moment. In the old world, the sales interaction is often fleeting and might not be verbal. Too often, this interaction is the hand that points to the right aisle, right shelf, or right product.

Digital changes the sales interaction and enables instant and rich collaboration if the brand is ready to take advantage of the opportunity. The same elements of two-way dialogue, both ongoing and momentary conversation, drive successful sales. However, in the digital landscape of these moments, the relationship and trust can flourish, evaporate, never appear, get tarnished, or fail to be connected due to the immediacy of our interactions. Think how quickly Allstate, IBM, and Zappos have to react and interact with a complex set of services, ideas, and customer inputs. Mortgage preapprovals that once took hours, days, or even weeks now happen in minutes or seconds. These are large personal or organizational decisions, and trust in the sales approach continues to matter in the decision-making process. This behavior indicates that trust is possibly the competitive advantage for sales. Marketing experts Don Peppers and Martha Rogers use the example of Ally bank, an entirely online banking institution that actively reminds customers that money that they have in certain accounts would earn higher interest rates if moved to other types of accounts. There is no charge for this model, and it represents a trust currency that enables the customer to get more value from their relationship with Ally than with other banks. This is what Peppers and Rogers refer to when they say that "trust and honesty are a competitive advantage." This example shows how digital and sales can be used together to deliver value beyond the sum of their individual parts. The Ally example shows what can happen after the relationship begins. But digital can and should be the linchpin that identifies and defines the sales interactions and brings together all the right components to build trust and get the customer to your side.

> "We're very focused on delivering experiences that are innovative, personalized, and frictionless to our members as well as proactive, wherever possible. This is important to us

as an organization from top to bottom in the way that we want to think about our members' relationship with USAA at every interaction. To do this, we must understand our members and their needs as well as, if not better than, they do themselves. We use this as our core to deliver very simple, reliable, focused, digital products that are supported by processes and interaction models that are all about making the experience robust and intuitive for our member base."

—Chris Cox, head of Digital Experience Delivery, USAA

The importance of digital's role in sales is further emphasized by the research we conducted. Fifty-six percent of respondents saw the number one opportunity for digital transformation as improving sales operations and customer satisfaction. Gaining a competitive advantage was next at 47 percent. These findings show that successful organizations recognize the need to shift the way they are leveraging and organizing the sales function around digital principles to improve customer success.

But how and where do organizations shift and change to build lasting, meaningful relationships with customers using digital? According to Peter Drucker and Theodore Levitt, the fundamental focus of an enterprise is to sell and market product and services. Old and simplistic as this sounds, it also does not account for the relationship and trust variables that drive effective sales or how to get that trust in a world of near-instant digital sales cycles. Being always on and omnipresent in the sales cycle is impossible for brands when you consider the pervasive digital universe of choices. Rather, successful organizations look for and optimize the key moments where leveraging trust can hold the buyer's attention and present an opportunity for sales. The key is to be the digitally transformed organization that can present itself at these critical moments when the buyer is ready to interact. So how do brands map these moments in the digital world and transform sales to be there and ready in the right way?

From our work and research, we see that leading Digital Helix organizations use three underlying factors that force sales to radically change the way they think, invest, and behave in building customer relationships.

Factor One

Customers, no matter the market or category, have extreme levels of control over the sales functions in a digital world. Everything is one click away. From abandoning a shopping cart to requesting more information to searching for alternatives to deciding to purchase, customers can go in any direction they see fit in less than a second. An interesting paradigm of digital in this situation is that the vast expansion in customer information gathering has also radically diminished the customer's desire to trust information until it is filtered in his or her own specific way. Now, most buyers use any combination of social, influencer, independent media, or even experientially driven information to verify and assess the information brands provide. It is this overwhelming task of search and evaluation that makes trust so critical for both brands and customers. Building trust becomes a shortcut in the digital journey, and it is an incredibly simple way to help when and where consumers want it in a world they control. Think back to the Ally bank example. If you trust Ally is always looking out for your best interests, where will you look first when a new banking opportunity arises?

Factor Two

Instead of having to get information in large buckets (brochures, websites, events, etc.), customers can get hundreds of small slices pulled together from digital sources that they find through their own cycles. It is nearly impossible for any marketing team to do it all or be everywhere. But if the sales team could be at the right moments with slices of the right information, there is a far higher chance for success. In fact, our research has shown that Gen X buyers consume five times as much information and content as baby boomers. Imagine how this impact will grow as more digitally savvy buyers get more information faster in the coming decade and are able to slice and paste their own tapestry of information instantly in a self-controlled purchasing cycle. Think how this might impact your sales and marketing functions. Do you have the right content slices (product, customer feedback, etc.) in the right places (social, search, with sales teams, etc.) when the moment hits your buyers to either further the relationship or build a new one?

Factor Three

The more other organizations move to embrace new sales processes, the more we will likely see a shift toward longer-term behavioral changes. Self-actualization by buyers of the whole sales process in connected moments around slices of information is already becoming the norm. Think about apps that enable instant price matching or Google ads that deliver information through search or retargeting to remind the buyer of deals they searched for. And this is just one section of the funnel. Buyers are now accustomed to seeing, digesting, and having slices of information presented wherever they are. This nonlinear journey can seem to be an almost chaotic combination of events, which is probably not fully understood by the customer. This digital sales journey is a rhythmic process nonetheless.

In most organizations, sales has been attempting to manage a linear model starting at awareness building and moving to consideration to preference to purchase. Many successful digital firms have realized that in too many cases long-term trust and happening to be at the right place at the right time with the right information is what ultimately drove the sale, not the careful linear sales model. In either B2B (where this is a more obvious dynamic) or B2C (where the challenge is the ability to intercept the buyer in the exact moment), the shape of successful selling and how trust is garnered in that process has changed forever.

Think about creating an infographic on the five questions to ask before buying a particular product. We produced such a chart on Lasik early on in our careers that discussed why each question was important and what buyers should look for in a provider. This positions other brands as proactive buyers and enables sales to enter at any moment with an educational slice of information to redirect the conversation to the brand. Does your organization have content like this that can be delivered digitally in a number of different moments by sales and marketing to build trust and demonstrate your brand's value?

You need to evaluate your organization's sales models and see where the company still relies on an old linear nature that is biased toward funnel management. This requires identifying a new patchwork of information and moments for sales to own and target. However, moving sales to a new digital framework can only be done in a connected organization that has the systems and culture available to enable the sharing of information across functions. For example, does your organization have the ability to see and track a download? Can you track a visit to a key sequence of web pages and connect that to a response of a specific advertisement? Can consumers purchase and then visit an additional product part of the website? Armed with information and the right automation in a system like Salesforce, your sales team could, with surgery-like precision, deliver the exact digital slices to the prospect to reinforce or build the trust the customer seeks. This is exactly what digital enables to its fullest. Digital gives your brand the ability to show that your organization understands the customer or prospect and their needs when and where it matters.

> "Digital transformation is centered on the relationship you want to have with your customers. Do you as a brand really understand what your customers want, how they are making new decisions, how they are going through their journey, and what they are trying to accomplish? Where do you meet them along that digital journey? Answering these questions correctly is becoming very lucrative for brands and also forces differentiation. So if I am a company that understands my customers' needs better, I anticipate them better, and I'm going to have an advantage over my competitors. In many ways, understanding your customers better prompts investing in content that gives you more touch points, which is key to any sort of sale. The better my touch point with my customer, the better we can sell to them. Digital is by far the best way to improve the sales process, in terms of the consistency and also the scalability."
>
> **—Charlene Li, principal analyst, Altimeter, a Prophet company**

To give you a more concrete understanding of this principle, figure 12.1 shows how the customer's or prospect's quest for information drives the new moments approach. It can be sequenced in three possible pathways (A, B, or C) in this example. But you cannot catch them all or be everywhere with either marketing or sales. We have heard a lot about the idea of social selling and the notion of being where your customers are when they are online. This is not what we are describing, and social selling is only one small but interesting component of the idea of sales moments. Rather, sales moments involve all forms of the customer's content or information needs and takes into account the concept of right time and place, no matter if it is offline or online.

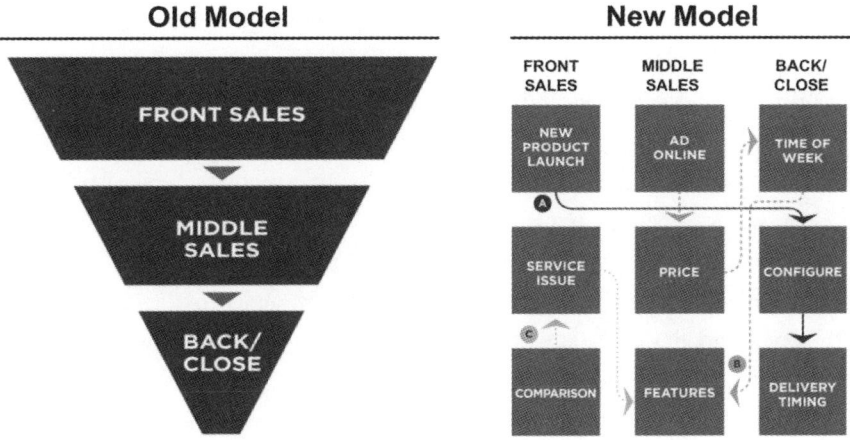

Figure 12.1: Old Sales Model vs. New in the Digital World

In both the B2C and B2B markets, brands need to leverage the concept that the customer has control. In this regard, you cannot change the direction of the wind, but smart organizations adjust their sails to reach the best destination faster. These adjustments allow organizations to take advantage of the natural forces of the customers' sales journey that enable winners to gain an advantage. By understanding how to respond and be where their customers are at key times and places, leading firms have exponentially increased their sales efficacy by delivering digital content for the exact moments that matter to their customers.

So what do moments look like? Well for one of our clients, looking over the data and interviewing sales teams and customers showed us that a vast majority of their sales happened in under sixty days. In addition, those over sixty days tended not to come to fruition anytime soon, if at all. In a traditional sales organization, the leadership might be tempted to figure out what can be done to improve the close rate on the over-sixty-day prospects. But data and research showed that customers were buying because they had an immediate need for our client's technology product. Just by luck, they had started selling how fast they could solve complex problems, not knowing most customers came to them in dire straits for a quick solution to a problem with a tight deadline. This is a moment. Knowing that prospects have dozens of other alternatives from the leading brands in the space for simple, long-term projects as well as understanding that our client can be the superhero for those extraordinary problems was a huge move forward.

Think about it. We no longer have to go toe to toe with larger, more established, and better capitalized brands. We can concentrate our sales and marketing on the moments that matter and where we have an advantage. We can produce digital content that helps people identify these situations, determine how best to handle them, and showcase key elements like customer feedback and profiles that show we are the obvious solution to whatever problem they are trying to solve. This approach provides clarity and efficiency and demonstrates that if we can help in your moment of crisis, we can also handle your day-to-day needs as well.

This last point is particularly important. Without having a broad market approach, we have built in a broad market strategy to use our advantage to grow the business by leveraging our superior ability to handle "even your most difficult challenges." Now our client can focus on the moment that matters for the customer, and they are uniquely suited to win, be where these moments arise online and off, and have a focused content effort that is within budget and sustainable. This approach, combined with sales training and automation in Salesforce, is enabling these companies to win in a space dominated by Fortune 500 brands with sales teams that outnumber them twenty to one.

To determine if your sales functions (as individual transactions or as relationship managers) are equipped to win, you will need to audit their capabilities against these key questions:

1. Have you tracked the moments that matter to your customers with your digital tools, surveys, and interviews so that your sales force can interact with customers and prospects in the most relevant moments?
2. Do you have feedback systems that constantly track the content needs and wants for customers around each of the moments that matter?
3. Can you adjust quickly to give sales new content or slices that are pertinent for a small window of time?

4. Have you created portfolios of content and information that can be used at will by sales functions for each of the moments?
5. Are you rewarding or measuring sales around their ability to amplify trust and deliver in the moments that matter?
6. Do you have systems to enable sales to automate and refine the content slices for each moment that matters?

> "If you looked at IBM before and after our transformation, you would see how we moved from hierarchical structure to agile, self-directed teams. Our teams are completely focused on the reality of what's happening in the market. If you're not driven by what's happening with your customers in the moment and how people are actually engaging and responding to you and your efforts, you have lost already."
> **—Jon Iwata, senior vice president, marketing and communications, IBM**

It is also important to know that shifting sales to digital can turn into an eternal debate if your market or markets buy based on one moment, some simple connected moments, or a complex set of interconnected moments. Moments matter more than ever before in sales functions because trust as a currency is swinging toward whether or not sales can aid or orchestrate these moments. Information systems aside, there are three key elements that will drive success here:

Identifying Moments

First you have to know when and what these moments for sales engagement can look like. As we discussed in our previous example, data and research can and will show you the moments that matter. What you want to be wary of is creating a whack-a-mole model where sales points out any possibility of nailing a moment by accident.

Moments are, by definition:

- Actionable: Meaning we as an organization see the opportunity and understand the logical next steps. For example, your organization should understand the difference in actions between seeing a change in a prospect's business that usually means a need to upgrade or change systems versus seeing the same change but knowing the prospect is under contract for two years and cannot change providers.
- Acknowledged by the customer: If we were to ask our customers, they would understand and agree that their need was specific and actionable—for example, needing more support or infrastructure during seasonal or peak times.
- Repeatable: There has to be a pattern of behavior or needs that can be seen over many customers and scenarios. For example, adding complementary products or entering a new market versus one-off manufacturing or staffing changes.
- Recognizable: We can set up rules to find it and take action on it—for example, leadership or other changes that are searchable or in the public domain via quarterly reports versus internal systems.

You will see that many of these criteria require some level of search or listening to understand. While much of this information can be somewhat easy to find, depending on your business, you may need to begin training sales and marketing to listen for the key elements that drive a purchase within your customers. Over time and with the right customer research, these moments and their triggers will become second nature for the organization, as they have become for many digital leaders today. As we pointed out, sometimes the moment that matters most to you is the one moment that you are best equipped to address. Not all companies are equal, and not all moments are perfect. Just because you have used the criteria to identify the moment does not mean it is the best or only moment for your business to win. In the digital world, as we have discussed, experimentation and research should be your guide.

Once you have your moment(s) identified, sales needs a set of moment playbooks to show them exactly what to do and when and where it matters. Execution and adjustment is critical at this step. Without the right playbooks, it is far too easy to resort back to linear, nondigital thinking and actions. Sales may not feel that they have the same historical controls as before (funnel management), but in reality, they are far better equipped to thrive with this method than by trying to force old methods into a new world.

Building the Right Systems

Systems have to be built to give extremely quick feedback on what is working and what is not working in terms of customer needs. It is far better in this environment to have 80 percent of what you need now than a 100 percent perfect view after the moment has passed. Whether it is a single, paired, or complex moment sell, sales needs to be empowered to make choices as fast as possible. They can adjust on a near-term basis, but if the moment passes, then it is lost. The CIO needs to be the chief sales officer's number-one partner. The social feedback systems from service and support as well as communications are the most vital tools they can have. But any and all feedback needs to be rapidly collected, filtered, and delivered so that this information can deliver a much closer set of interpersonal actions for an organization's customers. The sales function has to be far more intimately involved with the flow and analysis of information beyond pure revenue targets. In effect, great sales in the Digital Helix organization have more to do with how trust is built around the customers' needs when and where it matters than a stereotypical sales prospecting and responding approach. Relationships are crucial in this chaotic landscape, but the ability to partner with a customer in a transparent way is essential. There is logic for why Progressive Insurance so happily shows (and advertises) that you can get competitive quotes compared on their site with their own quotes. They understand the brevity of that comparative shopping moment, how to be there with the customer as it happens, and how to not lose them.

Aligning Culture

From a cultural perspective, it is vital that sales become even more highly indexed on listening than ever before. We started this chapter discussing how important relationships are in our world. In Digital Helix organizations, sales functions excel in identifying and working the moments that matter. They become instinctively better at gaining insights on how to maximize those moments. This is where the "Challenger" sales model from Dixon and Adamson's book *The Challenger Sale: Taking Control of the Customer Conversation* becomes the norm. In this book, the authors state that Challengers have a deep understanding of the customer's business and use that understanding to push the customer's thinking and teach them something new about how their company can compete more effectively. A Challenger is really defined by the ability to do three things: teach, tailor, and take control. These organizations focus on pushing the customer out of their comfort zone. This book is a great starting point because it talks about what it takes to be part of that conversation, especially in a world where their conversations might be very short.

Putting these three elements together is the key to transforming your sales function. As we have discussed, digital transformation requires you to do more than simply identify the right elements and put them in place. The organization and the structure of the company and its culture must reward and support the sales function to be truly successful. By building trust with your buyers, while understanding the moments that matter in their journeys, your organization can use sales to either elevate your transformation or begin to reap new benefits from being digital. How well does your organization know the value of each moment in the connected sales process?

CHAPTER 13

EVERYONE TOGETHER, ALL THE TIME

*"Innovation, the heart of the knowledge economy,
is fundamentally social."*
—Malcolm Gladwell

Some may wonder why company and team dynamics is one of the last pieces of the Digital Helix, especially since people and collaboration play such a crucial role in building the foundation of digital transformation. This decision was made not because this topic lacks importance, but rather because the foundational components of the helix need to be in place before you can think about how teams factor into the equation.

There are two key reasons why this topic is essential for digital transformation success. First, ongoing mutual support from teams as well as from individuals is critical to any successful organization. No leader would ever suggest otherwise. Yet all the research and interviews we have done point to how difficult it is to get and keep people working together and remaining responsible to each other. Due to the dynamic nature of digital, many find it more difficult than ever to ensure that everyone is watching each other's backs. Almost all people we have worked with and interviewed tell us that the traditional top-down ways of holding teams and projects together do not work at the level they did only a few years ago.

Think about the power of bringing people together to perform the functions of digital transformation within your organization. Digital enables everyone to listen better, share more, integrate activities, blur roles and functions, and experiment at will. This level of integration and flexibility is a different landscape from the traditional silo of departments so common in the less-digital age. A successful digital transformation requires strategic design sensibility around the components in the Digital Helix. This shift compels executives to begin seeing sales as moments and not journeys and to start understanding that strategy is often a moving dynamic. Each component of the business must understand that the organization is better served by harnessing the power of connecting people instead of just branching out as independent functions.

To allow this shift to happen, each individual and team needs to be aligned with the digital goals that enable everyone to thrive and succeed.

> "Organizations that take a 'network effects' approach to interaction design are the ones who 'get' it. They understand Tim O'Reilly's great insight that digital services should become more valuable the more people use them. That's 'more' as in the number of people and 'more' as in the amount of use. As a fundamental organizing principle for success, the technical and economic benefits of network effects are as true for Amazon recommendation engines as they are for Google search engines. The network effects approach requires that you design for collaboration and digital together and not merely try to digitize your organization to create the illusion of continuity. Organizations that understand digital transformation is an investment in network effects will find themselves far ahead of the others."
>
> **—Michael Schrage, research fellow at MIT Sloan School's Initiative on the Digital Economy, oversees research on digital experimentation and network effects, and is author of** *The Innovator's Hypothesis*

Effectively aligning teams with digital goals is an ongoing challenge. Executives in Fortune-type organizations told us in our research that the strongest benefits of successful digital transformation are increased competitive advantages (89 percent), improved external and internal collaboration (87 percent), and enhanced management of growth demands (87 percent). These benefits are only outcomes because they break the traditional silo approach that dominates traditional models. In more traditional models the focus on outcome rarely includes the need to change the way people work together after the needed outcome has occurred. Given the exponential changes in the digital world, focusing on processes is vital, especially because some outcomes are clearly not known. Leaders of digital transformation must think about how knowledge, interactions, and interchangeability are constantly tied together. This ecosystem thinking is a better measure of how goals can be achieved.

Second, for every new process that is introduced, there are several makeshift workarounds that people and teams employ to get their jobs done. These "systems" are hard to replace, as they have the owners' pride of authorship and development behind them. Often replacing these processes also carries risks. One example of a shift in process that most people know of is the agile development model. Agile was originally designed to remove the barriers to rapid software and service delivery in IT functions as the cloud and apps on demand became more prevalent. As we become more technology dependent with digital transformations, it is inevitable that some of the methods used to drive change in IT will migrate across the rest of the organization. In a *Harvard Business Review* (*HBR*) article entitled "Embracing Agile, How to Master the Process That Is Transforming Management,"[1] the authors talk about the factors that drive and prevent great success with Agile. They found that many companies that launch Agile projects fail because most people become overly involved in the work of individual teams, talk more than they listen, and promote marginal ideas that a team has previously considered and already put on the back burner.

> "We have redefined roles to be much more specialized and recast our people into 'Agile Squads.' We've assigned these squads to different parts of our business portfolio—either a geographic

unit, a country team, or a P&L unit or product unit. We then get these squads to come together as teams for a one-week, intensive boot camp. They learn about Agile and study both the new digital methods and the traditional methods, including how to create quality content. It's the combination of the two that has really gotten tremendous feedback. After the boot camp, they go back as Agile squads and apply their learning to their part of the business. They become self-directed teams that are driven by data and market realities. This is what makes the program and the squad very conducive to creativity and innovation. The improvement in their work is dramatic."

—Jon Iwata, senior vice president, marketing and communications, IBM

Even with the best intentions, these missteps erode the benefits that Agile innovation can deliver, as the model is built on a "cadre of eager participants." To succeed with the Agile model, as well as with digital transformation, organizations need to provide the right supportive environment while trusting employees to get the job done in the new model. As the *HBR* authors pointed out, "General George S. Patton Jr. famously advised leaders never to tell people how to do things: 'Tell them what to do, and they will surprise you with their ingenuity.'" Rather than give orders, leaders learn to guide with questions, such as "What do you recommend?" and "How could we test that?" This principle for success communicates, supports, and allows organizations to put people over processes and tools. Like the Digital Helix model, this framework has shown that it creates transformational results. Success can only happen if organizations, teams, and individuals let go of nondigital thinking and makeshift processes.

"Digital and the changes that it brings move at different speeds, and it's sometimes hard to fit the pieces together seamlessly without withdrawing or scaling back. Organizations and people should be cautious and focus on the areas where you have traction to move forward as opposed to pushing on those that are stalled. To get digital right, you must have the right approach,

which starts by getting people to come together in a different and stronger way that reinforces the digital goals, teams, and results. Look for low-risk starting points and a good general direction for how you're going to approach digital, and then you refine it and make it better every day with the help of the teams involved. This steady process is how you get people to realign to the new ways of digital and build a better, more agile workforce in the process."
—**Rick Holgate, former CIO, Bureau of Alcohol, Tobacco, Firearms & Explosives, current research director, Gartner**

To succeed in digital, leaders need to inspire unity of purpose, unity around information, and even unity over principles and practices. But in most large and established organizations, this collaboration happens mostly in small clusters, if at all. Startups, in contrast, tend to be digital by nature, which encourages more of an "all-for-one" mentality around a simple goal or objective. This singular-purpose mindset is essential to binding people to goals. In larger organizations, this binding is difficult due to progressively more complex structures, history, geography, and organizational complexities. As we have seen and the research proves, commitment to digital goals across teams with a startup mentality is essential for success. This commitment is where the concept of "all together or all for one, all the time" comes in. The mantra may sound blindly optimistic on the surface, but in a digital world where all actions can immediately affect others and decisions need to be made quickly, a common set of priorities is vital for action and results.

Strong teams are something that successful digital organizations know and understand, be it a small startup fighting to succeed and gain share or the largest retailer in the world. If you look at Amazon, you will see a company that acts like a startup at its core. The company uses its list of fourteen leadership principles to guide business decisions, as well as to guide the people, functions, and interactions across the organization. Anyone who looks at these fourteen principles will see they include several keys to getting teams to consistently come together and that they have helped Amazon become one of the most digital businesses on the planet. Read these principles and compare them to your environment. Think about how you would make decisions at Amazon and at your company if these were the fourteen things you hired on, evaluated people on, and based decisions on.

Digital Perspective

Here are the fourteen principles Amazon uses across its business and for hiring and evaluating its employees:

1. Customer Obsession

Leaders start with the customer and work backward to earn and keep customer trust.

2. Ownership

Leaders are owners and don't sacrifice long-term value for short-term results.

3. Invent and Simplify

Leaders expect and require innovation and invention from their teams and always find ways to simplify.

4. Are Right, a Lot

Leaders are right a lot. They seek diverse perspectives and work to disconfirm their beliefs.

5. Learn and Be Curious

Leaders are never done learning and always seek to improve themselves and be curious about new possibilities and act to explore them.

6. Hire and Develop the Best

Leaders raise the performance bar with every hire and promotion.

7. Insist on the Highest Standards

Leaders have relentlessly high standards—many people may think these standards are unreasonably high. Leaders are continually raising the bar and driving their teams to deliver high-quality products, services, and processes.

8. Think Big

Thinking small is a self-fulfilling prophecy. Leaders create and communicate a bold direction that inspires results.

9. Bias for Action

Speed matters in business. Many decisions and actions are reversible and do not need extensive study. We value calculated risk taking.

10. Frugality

Accomplish more with less. Constraints breed resourcefulness, self-sufficiency, and invention.

11. Earn Trust

Leaders listen attentively, speak candidly, and treat others respectfully. They benchmark themselves and their teams against the best.

12. Dive Deep

Leaders operate at all levels, stay connected to the details, audit frequently, and are skeptical when metrics differ. No task is beneath them.

13. Have Backbone; Disagree and Commit

Leaders are obligated to respectfully challenge decisions when they disagree, even when doing so is uncomfortable or exhausting.

14. Deliver Results

Leaders focus on the key inputs for their business and deliver them with the right quality and in a timely fashion.[2]

As you read these principles, notice they include topics such as ownership, invent and simplify, learn and be curious, think big, and a bias for action, among others. While this is a nice-sounding list, how these principles are used across the organization is more important than the words themselves. To quote Amazon, "Our Leadership Principles aren't just a pretty inspirational wall hanging. These Principles work hard, just like we do. Amazonians use them, every day, whether they're discussing ideas for new projects, deciding on the best solution for a customer's problem, or interviewing candidates. It's just one of the things that makes Amazon peculiar."[3] Having worked with Amazon directly, we can attest to the fact that these principles are in fact used every day to bind teams, direct actions, and push everyone to find new solutions together that are not readily apparent from a business-as-usual approach. In fact, while working with their B2B gift card group, together we revamped the sales motions, created new digital sales processes, and developed an entirely new digital content marketing and fulfillment system in less than four months. We saw firsthand how the fourteen principles and having the right teams removed barriers that would have stymied efforts elsewhere. While Amazon is not unique in this regard, they are a near-perfect example.

How do you ensure this level of binding in your organization? The secret is in the binding mechanism combined with a complete organizational support and enablement structure. While some may argue about which is more important—the rallying cry or the structure—research and experience show you need both in concert so that your teams can work across boundaries to achieve great things. If you look at any great organization, you will find that glue and a holistic structure supports it. The "glue" is the intrinsic bond that brings people and teams together for a common vision or cause, but it goes deeper as well. Looking back at Amazon, its goal is to be the "most customer-obsessed company."

Jeff Bezos has led that charge and inspired the vision and the steps to make that goal a reality, but it is the fourteen principles that guide the teams and people that help make the organization successful every day. As we have and will continue to discuss throughout this book, Amazon takes risks and experiments like no other company. This level of experimentation would not be possible without their leadership's commitment to hiring the right kinds of people and enabling and encouraging them to come together across every facet of the business to meet their goals. This simultaneously top-down, middle-out, and bottom-up way of getting teams and people working together is what Jeff Bezos calls a "pioneer spirit."

> "When you attract people who have the DNA of pioneers and the DNA of explorers, you build a company of like-minded people who want to invent. Creating is what they think about when they get up in the morning: how are we going to work backward from customers and build a great service or a great product? This innate curiosity is a key element to invention. This curiosity is the fun part, so if you're the right kind of person that likes to invent and make the world a better place, you're the type of person that excels at Amazon. Over the last eighteen-plus years, Amazon has attracted a bunch of people that have fun changing the game."[4]
>
> **—Jeff Bezos, CEO, Amazon**

Not every employee or team can adjust to a world where these principles are applied as a whole, or even in pieces. The power of the all-together approach is that it is fundamentally designed to bring everybody to the table as equals as long as they have access to the right information. Think back to the theme and stream examples we discussed and the new and immense opportunities that information and data are providing. People and teams that are finding new, creative, and innovative ways to harness this information are the stars. Those who love going down different roads just to figure out where they lead, even if they hit a few dead ends along the way, are the ones who drive successful digital transformations. This innate curiosity leads to a willingness to experiment, push boundaries, and ask questions that most don't ask. This mindset also leads to the creation of a binding that brings everyone together around a shared goal or vision.

The ability to be successful with digital transformation in your organization largely comes down to taking a fundamentally different approach to enabling people to work together in an empowered and informed way. A Digital Helix organization in action looks and functions like a startup or digital giant like Amazon in many ways. Becoming a Digital Helix organization starts during the hiring process and is constantly tested through a set of working principles that respect the role of teams and individuals to solve problems as they occur and evolve.

Hiring, coaching, and talent development become huge catalysts for digital. Like so many aspects of transformation, every department plays a role, and HR cannot be left out.

> "If you think about the many different industries where there is a consumer frustration with the legacy incumbent, you see one company trying to protect their position, their revenues, and their profitability streams. Companies find it difficult to move as they don't have a digital, innovative dynamic that thrives on change and finding new answers. These people are protective and don't want to upset the status quo within the business. They don't want to potentially lose their own job, so they move things along slowly to make sure that they're secure. The ones that succeed run in essence skunk works and use entrepreneurial-type groups that can go off to experiment and challenge the whole company. Apple was the master of this concept. Under Steve Jobs, the company would actually create completely different, independent units that were completely separate from the main business, whose job was sometimes even to destroy the main business. However, not many companies have the vision, leadership, or willingness to be able to do that. Unfortunately, for most organizations and leaders, it is easier to live in a culture that maintains the current status quo than to push toward change and build something new all of the time."
> **—Colin Crawford, investor, Loudr**

Every successful digitally transformed organization combines a boundary-pushing vision with an innovative culture backed by key principles that guide daily actions. Even if you get some or all of the other Digital Helix components right, without enabling people to function together in a digital-first world, your helix is neither complete nor effective. Listening differently, having executives who push digital barriers, seeing customers as having portfolios of experiences, and truly connecting sales', marketing's, and communications' views of the world means little without having teams with the right mindsets to use this new knowledge. As our research has shown, having 90 percent of the right elements is often no better than having 40 percent in place. This fact alone should push you to get 100 percent and not waste time getting most of the way there for far less of the benefits.

Think this statistic is an overstatement? Think about the digital leaders and laggards in the world today. By all accounts, Walmart should have beaten Amazon. GM should currently be the leader in electric cars, not Tesla. There are hundreds of other examples like this where once leading brands did not innovate people, processes, and products to remain ahead. Amazon is again a great example of digital success. The company began as a book retailer and is now the largest web host in the world. That level of innovation is only possible if your organization brings people across teams together to ask the right questions and encourage the answers to be explored, no matter what the answer turns out to be.

If you are a senior executive reading this, your role is to drive all the pieces of the Digital Helix together for maximum success. In just this one helix component, you should be able to see that executive leadership requires much more than just setting vision and providing encouragement. You and your organizations' leaders, teams, and people need more vital and innovative mindsets so that everybody can function at the pace of digital and continue to adapt to the change it brings. If you believe that humans are infinitely valuable to your organization's success, then your role has to be about bringing them together every day in every way, all the time.

As numerous articles and case studies[5] have pointed out, a shift is occurring in talent management from one that focuses on outcomes to one that is more focused on learnings. The key finding is that organizations have learned that their focus when teaching problem-solving skills and developing people has to be on teaching those skills and the ability to handle a constantly changing world. Digital transformations are, at their heart, human development opportunities. With access to capital, technology, and information being more abundant than ever, the challenge is less about finding talent than it is about knowing how to filter it and use it to drive transformation.

The challenge is bringing people and teams together in the same way that new digital information comes together from disparate places and moments within and from outside the organization. For this to happen, we need to make sure our people are up for and ready to adapt as the needs arise and change. "All together" is a key component in this success. If you hire, train, and enable people to be together all the time in how they work with the same ease we now move data across functions and roles, we will be successful. What one element can bring groups together in the next thirty days?

CHAPTER 14

IN THE MOMENT AND ONE STEP AHEAD ALWAYS

"It is a mistake to look too far ahead. Only one link in the chain of destiny can be handled at a time."
—Sir Winston Churchill

As we have seen in our work as well as in the work of numerous others, people and organizations promote and reward based on past performance. But in a digital world, past performance often has little or nothing to do with future success. In fact, agility and willingness to experiment are important traits in digital leaders, and past performance metrics can often be gamed to inflate success. When companies focus on performance and volume or sales metrics to the exclusion of other measurements, many individuals will provide lower goals. They know they can hit these numbers and will be rewarded and even applauded for "exceeding expectations." Surveys have even shown that two-thirds of employees tell colleagues that they set goals that they are "sure they can meet." This play-it-safe behavior, both at the individual and at the organizational level, creates an environment where risk is avoided, experimentation is frowned upon, and underpromising while overdelivering is the unwritten rule for success.

"A culture that supports execution must recognize and reward other things as well, such as agility, teamwork, and ambition. Many companies fall short in this respect. Agility requires a willingness to experiment, and many managers avoid experimentation because they fear the consequences of failure. Half the managers we have surveyed believe that their careers would suffer if they pursued but failed at novel opportunities or innovations. Trying new things inevitably entails setbacks, and honestly discussing the challenges involved increases the odds of long-term success."[1]

—**Donald Sull, Rebecca Homkes, and Charles Sull**

Thinking about agility versus past performance and risk-taking versus consistency are just some of the key questions we will all face time and time again in the new digital world. The tension between these choices is due to the focus on efficiency and repetition versus a focus on the opposite, which comes with more potential risk and some levels of uncertainty. Alignment and execution become a priori needs for many executives, and in key moments the strategy often focuses everyone on one clear and long-term direction. Leaders must set up the culture and mindset of the organization so it can provide the foundation needed for digital success. Otherwise, tweaking the culture and living with the existing pre-digital mindsets that exist in every organization become the unseen barrier that will relegate your company to being an underachiever.

The ability to handle collaboration and the acceptance of the fact that no one strategy is perfect are fundamental to understanding how digital is different at its core from the old-world bias toward efficiency.

When we have gone into organizations that are in the process of moving toward digital, we have seen the tendency to handle stress by focusing on one issue and solution rather than developing alternative strategies upfront. In a digital environment, constant collaboration in design, delivery, reflection, and metrics can be a challenge for an organization used to a traditional single-focus approach. Beyond being challenging, this thinking and action puts an even greater stress on organizations looking to make transformative changes. If your focus, culture, and rewards systems favor doing the same things as before but with some small improvements, you are still 180 degrees from transformation.

David Lee, COO and CFO of Impossible Foods, stated during a McKinsey roundtable discussion on digital culture that "the true measure of agility is what businesses you have seeded to replace the business that is dying. Often the timing doesn't work. Transformations take a long time. It's a fallacy to look at the initial results. Rather, look at the underlying businesses that have high prospects for growth versus the ones that are dying."[3] This statement sums up one of the reasons many more companies fail at digital transformation than succeed regardless of the challenge. Revolution cannot occur without the bias toward evolution being broken by pushing, enabling, and encouraging extraordinary change that comes from accepting risks and moving to where the world soon may be, not where it will be tomorrow.

In our research, we have seen that success comes from understanding that there is no one perfect strategy for delivering digital transformation results. A constantly moving world with shifting market dynamics requires a new philosophy combined with a strategy that aims to be one step ahead and continuously evolving. Think about the set of variables your organization has to contend with within your market and company as well as assets and liabilities that are truly unique to your organization at any time. Long-term planning is too limiting and forces companies into a false "right path forward." You have to look ahead, watch trends, and adapt as needed. Planning needs to be based on a guiding framework for dealing with this variability. While it may sound nebulous and counterintuitive, there are patterns for this framework planning that we have seen in our own research and the work of others that will help you build this capability in your organization, now and moving forward.

Leading organizations consistently perform three elements of alternative strategy development that are tough to copy but essential to success:

1. Being constantly open to evolution
2. Designing alternative strategies with extensive experimentation
3. Building large advocacy and support groups (see the section "Digital Takes a Village and an Architecture" in chapter 5)

These three elements set the tone for digital leaders and create a foundation that moves beyond a single issue or long-term focus, which we have discussed. Successful teams and companies are driven to be one step ahead and constantly open to evolving their approach, tactics, and focus as the situation warrants. Even the mere openness to identify new possible paths (usually from the top with an executive as a digital explorer) sets the stage and provides the entire organization with the freedom and liberty to push limits and evolve. In truly successful firms, like Zappos for example, this way of thinking is part of the culture and DNA of the organization. Zappos and others who adopt and internalize this mindset see evolution as the most natural and best way to use their knowledge to push the boundaries of the business and their opportunities. These organizations train their people and teams to think about what is next and what borders are possible.

> "To move toward a new digital foundation, you stop feeding the old system you are using. You need to start right now with small customizations and programs that show the right style and right way forward. Once the results start flowing in, it opens your team's eyes to what's possible in their world and the whole of the business."
> —Jud Barr, president, JTB Consulting, LLC

Another key ingredient in most successful digital and social transformations is that leading brands deliberately design alternative strategies and do extensive experimentation before they commit to an initial kickoff. As we have mentioned, digital enables experimentation like never before. The ability to source, test, validate, and propose "what ifs" can happen quickly, easily, and immediately before an organization must fully commit. It is in these quick one-off moments that winners find the strategies, tactics, features, and insights that are worthy of full organizational support and resources. In success and in failure, these tests are illuminating for what they reveal to a keen digital enterprise. Look at Google. We have marveled at dozens of their successful experimentations and derided many of their failed attempts. But every success and every failure provided data and insights to improve their business and keep them one step ahead. While Google Glass did not take off, the knowledge about mobile use, activities, and patterns for connected devices is already helping them in ways that are not readily apparent to the end user.

In addition to having the openness to evolve and the willingness to experiment, there also needs to be a built-in advocacy and support system to bring ideas to fruition. Having the desire and ideas means absolutely nothing if the resources and wherewithal to incubate and grow are not robust enough to make the dream a reality. Organizations must go beyond simply changing attitudes. Yes, the company and key individuals have to be supportive. But there needs to be time, resources, and opportunity to plan and push for evolution as well. Far too often, great ideas die, or in the Internet economy become stand-alone ventures that should have helped propel or give needed insights to their corporate parents.

> "The mark of a great leader is when people in the organization interact with the head of the organization, do they feel smarter or do they feel stupider? Great leaders are seen as leadership 'geniuses' when they make individuals feel smarter and inspire them to push their vision forward. The challenge comes; does that vision empower us to collaborate, share, explore, and experiment in different ways?"
>
> —**Michael Schrage, research fellow at MIT Sloan School's Initiative on the Digital Economy, oversees research on digital experimentation and network effects, and is author of** *The Innovator's Hypothesis*

In today's world, brands must live up to customers' high standards, providing consumers with fast, free, instant delivery as well as numerous other amenities. The ability of companies to provide this retail experience came from experiments within Amazon. Before Amazon offered free shipping on orders over $25, any retailer would've told you that the math and economics don't work to support this. But differentiation and being one step ahead with customer desires pushed the company to run the experiment. Not surprisingly, Amazon found that Super Saver Shipping (as Amazon refers to it) on orders over $25 (which has since been changed to

$35) did not make good economic sense in the short term. But they asked a different question around customer values and brand loyalty. Using these metrics as a guide, the company saw free shipping dramatically pays off in both amount and frequency of purchases, thus increasing the lifetime value of almost every customer. All these delivery innovations could have come from other retailers or even shipping companies like FedEx or UPS. Being open, experimenting, and having the right internal structure enabled Amazon to build differentiation while keeping themselves one step ahead of the competition trying to copy them. Amazon is now looking into drones as a strategy to rewrite how delivery is done without using shippers as middlemen. The company is even piloting a program to deliver packages directly to the trunk of your car by partnering with Audi and DHL. Amazon recently introduced their Internet-connected "Dash" devices, which let you order items from an enormous online store with a single press of a button. The product has been wildly successful and has seen a 50 percent increase in use in just the first year. This level of success happens when the organization is set up right to take advantage of evolutions and revolutions simultaneously.

> "Experimentation can be a precursor to innovation, so make sure that you're always experimenting."[4]
> —Jeff Bezos, CEO, Amazon

One significant advantage of this combination of commitments is the ability to deliver new social and digital transformative programs twice as fast as organizations without alternative strategy models or extensive experimentation. From our own work and research, we have seen program launches happen more than twice as fast (75 days versus more than 150 days) than for those who do not adopt this mindset. Moving twice as fast not only brings speed but also provides the ability to run twice as many programs and gain advantages over the competition. In addition, organizations with this approach can also adjust strategy even more quickly by taking a greater range of inputs and outputs from their programs. In this case, speed kills the competition if it is organized properly. Digital leaders understand and think as much about the strategy as how to corral the right resources to constantly be pushing to be one step ahead.

But this speed and power is not unlimited. Even in the digital world with the promise of almost infinite scalability, it does not mean that each strategy or set of tactics is infinitely scalable. This is an important paradox to comprehend. In a world of increasingly gray strategic choices, the psychological tendency is to grab onto something and ride whatever it is until it is exhausted. But this strategy is not one step ahead. In reality, leaders in digital transformation are extremely aware of the need to continue to push boundaries and not accept hunkering down in one place, even when something is working. Going back to the Amazon example, even when free shipping was working, the company was busy developing Prime to speed up shipping and provide more value in the form of downloads. Shipping is just one part of the total offering, and according to Amazon, Prime is one of their most effective worldwide marketing tools.[5]

It is also important that we talk about measurement here. While experimentation and openness to evolution are critical, having the right objectives and metrics in place cannot be understated. As an organization, you need to be able to define what constitutes success. As we have discussed, this has to occur even after failures. But to accomplish this, the company and leadership must have the right framework for not only what to measure but also what insights or information they hope to gain before venturing down the path. If an experiment is done right and for the right reason, there will always be some form of victory, even in defeat. But you have to know what to look for before you get there.

> "Based on the work I do at MIT, both as a teacher and as an advisor to organizations, I can tell you that the quality of analytics in an organization is either a driver or barrier to results. The ability to hone in empirically, analytically, and experimentally on your best customers and your most likely prospects has really dramatically improved. Companies that choose to be data-driven in sophisticated ways (we are likely talking about no more than the top 10 or 15 percent of organizations) get a rapid accrual of benefits that are transformative. These organizations know

what to focus on in the myriad of choices to get to both the most efficient and effective way of investing for their customers, market, product portfolios, and overall business."

—**Michael Schrage, research fellow at MIT Sloan School's Initiative on the Digital Economy, oversees research on digital experimentation and network effects, and is author of** *The Innovator's Hypothesis*

Digital transformation winners understand the need for the right combination of strategies. For example, in effective digital and social transformations, "Thrivers," or social media leaders, routinely commit to only four types of eighteen social content strategies available. They focus on training, stakeholder Q&A, product strategy, and executive communications to thrive and stay ahead. Others, who are less successful, tend to use many more. Leaders recognize that a great content strategy is about a unique combination of ideas and the right combination of approaches. These executives understand that focusing only on one area or even naturally complementary areas, like crisis management and executive communications, cannot deliver the results desired the way the right palette of strategies can.

"Greatness requires deep focus on the right factors and right elements. Understanding and fine-tuning where to spend your time and energy is quite literally the difference between being great and average."

—**Dr. Michael Gervais, consultant to world-class athletes and teams, cofounder, Compete To Create Consulting**

To be successful with digital transformation you need a strong attachment to the Digital Helix as this philosophy plays itself out across the other six components in the framework. For example—

- Leaders should always be pushing the boundaries of great performance, both in the speed of execution and the constant quest of envisioning what is next.

- New information sources and identifying new ideas are essential to helping push the boundaries of what is next strategically.
- Focusing constant attention on the key elements of the customer's experiential portfolio enables organizations to not just execute better, but also to identify and naturally step ahead toward the next strategic opportunity.
- Marketing and communications should leverage their flows to identify and tap into potential next steps.
- Sales moments become more immediately understandable if we are looking for how they are evolving.
- These components can only work if the organization's collective involvement in knowledge and processes comes together and everybody is responsible to each other.

This is a severe departure from the old world where the idea of "in the moment" historically offered insights about being more efficient. The digital world sees "in the moment" as more about learning what an organization can or should do, not do, and how to gauge performance potential to move forward. This shift in understanding and a focus on constant change is at the center of successful digital transformations. Think about it this way: You can't be "one step ahead" if you don't know the alternatives. These alternative options need to be planned before and in parallel to activities that organizations are doing now. Companies also need to be open to building on these alternatives as the situation warrants and on an ongoing basis.

> "Many companies go after alternatives looking for the data they need like it is a needle in a haystack. With the gobs and gobs of data out there, trying to find the right data that makes sense at any moment in time is a challenge that distracts teams and leaders. Many organizations tend to wallow in the noise. The best companies work to find the right signal-to-noise ratio, and most start with a pretty simple premise to guide them. Using a customer-centric or customer-first approach and pushing to find alternative ways to deliver new value to the customer is their

'secret sauce.' Looking at all the enablers within the company, being open to off-beat options, and having the right digital tools can enable all of us to do that a lot more and stretch ourselves to deliver the next big thing for our customers."

—Colin Crawford, investor, Loudr

Now go back to the question we asked earlier about whom you would promote. Would you still choose the person who has executed flawlessly time and time again or the person who has pushed boundaries? In fact, most organizations need both great strategists and great executors. But since many companies still default to old paradigms, the question stands as a clear example of how many create false choices. To be one step ahead and in the moment, you clearly need a balance between the skills of the two candidates, plus a capacity to ask why (to identify the alternatives) in order to execute faster with digital knowledge as the guide.

Digitally transformed corporations also have the ability to constantly ask questions and get feedback from multiple parties to determine the next set of alternative strategies the organization should be looking into. This ongoing search for new answers can put enormous pressure on the organization to execute. But as with each of the other six digital DNA components, looking ahead is vital for highly successful and sustainable transformations. The capacity to be effective and stay one step ahead is often why digital startups can better adjust to the current world; they inherently live in the moment and often can only think of the next logical step.

A clear example of how this thinking manifests itself comes from a job interview early in one of our careers. The recruiter for a Fortune 100 brand asked a question designed to be calculated in one's head and to see how a candidate thinks. The question provided a set of parameters and focused on the resources needed to harvest a set of fields. According to the interviewer, the correct answer was 196 harvesters. When asked how the hell somebody could justify buying or leasing nearly 200 harvesters, let alone parking, manning, and even coordinating them, he was left dumbfounded. Using 196 harvesters cannot be the most efficient way to accomplish any task. Yet, in the moment and given strict rules and information, 196 was the right answer.

Increasingly, long-term strategies must not rely solely on the time-honored parameters we always use or default to. As we have discussed, almost every successful startup that has achieved scale over the last decade or so has redefined the boundaries by thinking about what is possible. From FedEx looking at overnight delivery by shipping everything to Memphis first to Uber redefining the pay-for-transportation model, companies that look one step ahead have and will continue to change what is possible and profitable. In the digital world, there will always be one or more teams looking to change the question, the frontiers, and the thinking in order to gain an advantage or launch a new business that eats into existing ones. The question is, will you be the one changing the question or the one being eaten into?

CHAPTER 15

BUILDING OPTIMAL MINDSET AND CULTURE

"An organization's ability to learn, and translate that learning into action rapidly, is the ultimate competitive advantage."
—Jack Welch

Even with all the right moves, investments, and strategies, digital does not work if the organization is not prepared to support it culturally. While there are any number of ways you can have or build a great culture inside your business, digital requires a digital culture mapped to the needs and priorities of an accelerated and constantly informed business. Digital is the engine for business success, and culture is the fuel to keep it running at top speed.

Research conducted by ourselves and others has consistently shown that no matter how much you transform your business, you have to have the right culture to reap the rewards. Winners build digital cultures across all elements of culture (vision, values, practices, people, narrative, environment, and many others) to provide the basis for success. Think about what this means for your organization when you factor in the Seven Drivers,

Seven Challenges, and Digital Helix components. For example, think about how the right culture is needed to support new digital metrics. These metrics help guide the business and require new forms of thinking and acting to capitalize on their results.

Organizations need to have the right digital culture that encourages openness to thinking about alternative strategies upfront and that allows extensive experimentation along the way. How many of us have worked for a great company that did not support and reward this behavior across the organization? And this is just one aspect of a digital business. A case could be made for all of the challenges, drivers, and Digital Helix components.

> "Digital requires rigorous thinking and an acceptance that your cultural norms have to change."
>
> **—Michael Schrage, research fellow at MIT Sloan School's Initiative on the Digital Economy, oversees research on digital experimentation and network effects, and is author of** *The Innovator's Hypothesis*

The key to getting any culture right, especially a digital one, is empowering individuals on a daily basis to put themselves into a more optimal mindset. The fact that much of the success winners experience is owned and managed from within suggests that peoples' skills and mindsets are vital ingredients for success. Leaders and department heads have to enable this transition in thinking and acting to make digital transformation a reality.

> "Everyone wants really highly successful people, functioning at their best and delivering really good results. This takes a commitment to the right culture. When introduced to new people, settings, and ways of doing things, there's a transition period. The organization has to be committed to teaching the ideas, the concepts, the principles, and the beliefs and showing what great looks like. To succeed, you have to find people with the right mindset to pass on the message and the mentality to maintain it and support it. We start by trying to make people appreciate and understand that the new philosophy is really valuable and a great way to elevate performance, re-create success, and establish the

foundation for the long term so everyone and the organization can function at their best."
—**Pete Carroll, head coach, Super Bowl Champion Seattle Seahawks**

This is a huge shift. For the better part of three hundred years, human capital and function has centered on the primary value of people being siloed in specific functions or departments. That was the power of economies of scale and the process that Adam Smith promulgated in *The Wealth of Nations*. People were a part of the system, not necessarily the system itself. But even with Smith's breakthrough in thinking, it is not uncommon today to see old-world cultural elements in digital-era organizations.

"The biggest risk is not taking any risk . . . In a world that is changing really quickly, the only strategy that is guaranteed to fail is not taking risks."[1]
—**Mark Zuckerberg, founder and CEO, Facebook**

To get to the level of optimal mindset, you must dive into the heart of how you help develop the people and culture in your organization. The key is to build a high-performance culture with diverse teams and individuals. This is no easy feat and requires new skills, mindsets, and knowledge for leaders and teams alike. One of the world's leading practitioners in cultural transformation in high-performance environments is psychologist Dr. Michael Gervais, consultant to world-class athletes, teams (including the Super Bowl champion Seattle Seahawks), and Fortune 100 corporations undergoing massive digital transformation changes. He has helped teams and individuals set themselves up for the creation and ongoing fueling of optimal mindsets in highly complex and competitive environments.

His expertise is invaluable, as he has succeeded in transitioning both teams and individuals from good to great and has helped people do things they might have never imagined to be possible. This is the promise of digital transformations. Remember, less than 20 percent of businesses get digital transformation right and see an economic benefit. The difference in winning and losing in a market or against a competitor often comes down to a handful of moments that make or break the quarter or the season. In addition, pro sports, the NFL in particular, are some of the most competitive and fast-paced environments in the world. Teamwork and performance matter every second of every day, including during practice. This is the world Dr. Michael Gervais excels in and helps others to succeed in even when faced with world-class competition. He, perhaps better than anyone, understands how to shift the psychology of your organization and capture the innate capacity of your most important asset, your people.

We asked Dr. Gervais a series of questions about high performance designed to understand what the key components of an organization need to look for to be successful now and in the future.

Question 1: What are the characteristics of organizations that seem to be able to make these cultural and high-performance leaps from where they are now to where they're heading?

"Over the course of being in the trenches with some of the most dynamic performers in the world, there are some common traits we see, from the environment they work in to their team setting to their internal makeup. One of those characteristics is a deep, deep curiosity toward mastery. There is an obsession with driving forward and mastering a process. At the core level, I've found that people are highly engaged in improvement. That deep drive toward mastery, with a curiosity of how to become better on a relentless basis, is one of the core factors allowing teams and individuals to continue growing. As soon as somebody becomes locked in, or they are smacked in a place where they have all of the answers, then we find stagnation and they stop growing. So, the first variable is this deep, intrinsic interest in growth and curiosity about mastery.

"The second variable is that people have a command of themselves. More specifically, they are able to handle themselves in quiet moments, rugged moments, and very hostile moments. This ability comes from having a rich awareness for who they are, how they express what they're working to develop, and how they express their craft. It sounds like a mouthful, but this approach and awareness helps individuals interface with their dynamic environments. If you couple the deep awareness they have about experiencing a moment-to-moment basis with a deep hunger and curiosity of how to grow and get better and progress, the combination tends to be an accelerant for sustained performance."

Question 2: How do people learn to take risks?

"This likely comes from the way our parents first taught us about learning, and there is one of two ways where this at least takes place. If our parents were hypercritical of the way we took risks, then we might learn something about the process of learning, since risk-taking is required to learn. Expressing or demonstrating what we've just learned is part of the risk-taking process. Environments that truly value when people take risks help people become curious and interested in what might be, as opposed to being fearful of what might not work right."

Question 3: When you look at this at an organizational level, is it fairly easy to understand which leaders have both the capacity and the desire for taking risks, and also the propensity for handling failure?

"For companies, I think that the ecosystem is naturally orientating toward capacity for curiosity or the propensity to handle failure. Startups are more interested in rapid iteration and in getting it right. But they also have a tolerance for making mistakes because the idea or ideology is to get something into the world. On the other hand, large and established companies have a history of winning and tend to play it safer. These large organizations focus more on accountability and metrics. This concentration is deeply embedded into the ecosystem, and thus more caution exists for employees, managers, directors, and leaders because if they make mistakes, the errors are likely recognizable and are often not understood by the organization."

Question 4: If you are the CEO of a Fortune-type organization and you're facing prototypical new-world pressures from agile startups, how do you incubate and then solidify potential test examples of successful digital transformations?

"What I've come to learn is that whether we refer to a startup, a large corporation, an individual athlete, or a collective team, human performance is met by our most precious and fragile resource: time. We need to get our arms around the idea that time, meaning this moment, is our most precious resource. Also, we need to understand that time is extremely fragile, because as we are talking, the last moments that first started this conversation are now gone. Time is the vehicle in which we experience life and relationships, and performance is expressed. If we can help our individual performers increase the quality and the frequency in which they experience moments, then a dramatic increase in output will result. The pace and the current way of living right now occur at unprecedented speeds. We're in the midst of an evolutionary adaption. This adaptation is forcing people to shut out irrelevant information in our time-compressed, rapid-paced life and business environment. Those who are able to shut out this irrelevant information will have a competitive advantage to perform optimally in environments that naturally have challenges. We are in a fast-paced environment where changes occur at an unprecedented pace. We, as leaders, need to train people's minds to better adapt to being in chaotic environments."

Question 5: Can we train mental skills so that we have the ability to perform under pressure in these fast-paced environments?

"There are many mental skills that we know are trainable. The discipline of sport psychology has taken a scientific approach to understand how world-leading performers train their mind to excel in pressure-packed environments. In the global business world, there is a sleeping giant that, once awake, will create a distinct competitive edge for employees and leaders. This advantage is not just about performing better during high-intensity contexts, but rather teaching and training the minds of the employees to be able to use the speed and pace of the modern-day workforce to their advantage.

"The pace and speed of modern business only becomes problematic if we lack the mental skills to thrive in those environments, or if we are not recovering well enough to be able to sustain the required output.

"It is not the actual speed of business; it is the pressure that we experience that prevents us from operating in real time. Pressure is the force that creates the belief that we have to think or do something faster than we might be capable of. For some people, the fast-paced environments are accelerants to performance. Those folks benefit mostly from training the mind to recover well. For some, the speed of the global business becomes a barrier to performance because it applies pressure to the mindset of the performer."

Question 6: What are some common pressures people face that hinder their performance?

"Pressure comes from fear of criticism, performance expectations, fear of looking bad, as well as the natural demands of deadlines and presentations. Most people are highly motivated to perform well but have not been taught or given the chance to properly train their mind so that they can excel in situations where they typically feel anxiety, tension, agitation, or straight-up panic. It seems absurd that we would train our craft (creating beautiful content for a presentation, for example) and not train our mind (having command of ourselves during that presentation), but therein lies the opportunity."

Question 7: What are ways that people can train their minds to excel in the modern-day conditions of global business?

"First, make a decision. Make a decision to train your mind so that you can live an authentic life more freely and more often. Once this decision is made, with a real commitment, you are on your way. Now the search for the most effective methods to train your mind begins.

"Second, train your mind to become more aware of the thoughts that build an optimal internal state for you. Invest in those thoughts by purposefully guiding your mind to one of these two types of thoughts: positive thoughts that are backed by real experiences in your past and give you the right to know that you can do difficult things in this moment. This is a commitment to be very clear about the types of thoughts that fuel the best version of yourself, that come from real experiences in your past.

"Third, just breathe. While you are becoming more aware of your thoughts, start becoming more aware of your internal activation level. The best way to think about activation levels is to imagine a scale from 1–10, with a 7, 8, 9, or 10 representing too much internal energy to perform and think optimally. An example of a 10 would be physically shaking right before a performance or presentation. On the other hand, on this scale, a 1, 2, or 3 is not having enough activation to be able to think optimally. An example of a 1 would be just getting out of bed. To have control over your activation level, just breathe. Deep breathing sends signals to the survival centers of the brain that we are safe. Deep breathing well is a trainable skill, and makes an immediate impact on finding an optimal activation level.

When people are consistently too low on the scale, it might be an indicator that they have not recovered well.

"Lastly, recover like a world-class performer. Getting adequate sleep, eating healthy, drinking water, and incorporating more movement in your day are all part of a recovery plan for people to be able to wake up consistently with fire, zeal, and zest."

Question 8: Walk us out five, maybe ten years from now. These changes in the work world and even at home feel exhausting. How much is fatigue an issue in driving these types of changes?

"To be good or even great at something, an incredible amount of time, energy, passion, grit, and deep focus needs to be crafted. To do all of this, an exorbitant amount of fuel is required. What's amazing about the human experience is that we can do difficult things for long periods of time, but every organism is bound by the same constraints of stress and recovery. There is an interesting paradox here, which we need to overcome to make digital transformations work. It's like the workforces of many world-class organizations are fatigued. This is because they and the organization have pushed so hard to handle the pace of information coming in at its current and ongoing pace. There is a ratio between deep curiosity and interest of mastery for not only finishing the job now but also doing it right to prevent penalization, demotion, or the chance of being fired. I believe that we need to be careful and mindful of the current working conditions, which require incredible amounts of energy from employees to become great. With the pace at which we're driving without the necessary recovery mechanisms to sustain such a high level, I fear we're going to find that our fatigue in many of these workplace environments will turn into deep staleness. This staleness results directly from not managing the recovery process well. By definition, staleness means that there's a lack of zeal, zest, spunk, and life in daily engagements, both in the workplace and at home. I can only imagine how this boredom would affect the cost of creativity, innovation, and progression.

"On the other hand, there is a potential upside for those that get ahead of this current fatigued workplace. If an organization can become aware and care about the possibility of fatigue, then the opportunity is very exciting. In a sporting context, if two talented teams are going to be competing and one is highly fatigued and not in an optimal state and the other is recovered and finely tuned, then the well-recovered team is going to have a competitive advantage. Like in business, this is where the gap between competitors becomes easily noticed and winners start to separate themselves. I think that a fork in the road will develop, separating successful organizations from laggards. Those that understand the value of human capital and the recovery process will be able to deliver sustainable and optimal performance."

Question 9: What two guiding principles do these changes lead us to think about?

"Number one, the highest-performing individuals, athletes, and organizations embrace the combination of taking risks and failure hand in hand. This appears to break many of the codicils of twentieth-century corporations.

"Number two, in a world where risk and the ability to decide how to manage information that matters (signals) versus information that doesn't matter (noise), filtering will help decide who wins and who does not. But this can only happen if these individuals are in a healthy workforce that is not too fatigued to see the differences when it matters."

If human capital is at the heart of the most successful digital transformations as we, Dr. Michael Gervais, and numerous others suggest, then we need to cultivate and enable it. Encouraging the capacity to strive for achievement through the rapid prototyping of ideas (alternative strategies) and actions (new ways to combine certain forms of execution) are essential nourishing mechanisms for the digital transformation process. Having the time to become more curious and to continue a thirst for learning might be the fuel your teams need. We encourage you to think hard about four high-performance and cultural development questions as you move forward at an ever-increasing pace in your digital transformation journeys:

1. Have you helped develop a new, more robust culture encouraging the fundamental acceptance of the need to accept and encourage experimentation as well as relevant failures?
2. Do you help your teams siphon or filter information from noise and focus on key signals?
3. Are you thinking about how to balance the energy levels and recovery

cycles needed for people increasingly stressed by constant change and rapid pace?

4. Are you investing in people and their ability to train the mental skills needed to perform at a high level?

If you want a true digital transformation to occur and not just a digital repackaging of current business practices, then the soul of your organization and how you reward, stimulate, and encourage people has to change. Acceptance of failure and having a high index for the capacity to learn and adjust is vital. The Digital Helix benefits we discussed can only be delivered through a fundamental change in the mindset and behaviors of organizations at an individual and collaborative level. In fact, each of the seven Digital Helix components collectively demands other underlying evolutions.

Following we define how critically changing mindsets and cultures are essential for success across the Seven Digital Helix components.

Executives as Digital Explorers

The key mindset shift here is the constant need to push boundaries outside of comfort zones within the unknown areas of the business and digital economy issues. The executive needs to have the right mindset to lead around these new principles and empower his or her teams to be mindful and able to handle the growth and pace required. Digital transformation involves changes in decade-old underlying assumptions, as well as the capacity to handle failure and potential ambiguities as we learn far more on the fly. The capacity to challenge age-old assumptions engrained in formal and informal learning is vital. The executive needs to let go of the instinct to control and lead more by exploring and filtering the good from the bad information as it happens. The new optimal mindset for the executive is leadership through learning, collaboration, and speed with experimentation.

Theme and Stream

Information is quite different in the Digital Age. Great digital transformations require that organizations know how to handle the constant underlying evolution of the value of information born from experimentation.

Changing mindsets to see information in connected versus eureka moments requires a confidence to break out from the abundance of noise and volume and to live in moments as they occur. This shift requires a stillness that can only come from developing a more optimal and high-performance mindset. It is so difficult to train ourselves to ignore information, but that is now part of the success factors we need to adopt and embrace if we want to thrive with digital. Knowing when to abandon or recategorize the value of information is also vital. This also requires a level of risk-taking, which is encouraged but rarely rewarded, and is now essential for success.

Customers Have Experiential Portfolios

Information is coming from everywhere: the Web, social, sales, customer service, friends, partners, etc. There might be hundreds, possibly thousands of inputs that change in value for customers and for us over time. Customers are aware of all these stimuli and in fact have developed radically different levels of high-performance mindsets to handle them well. To give you some perspective, the average consumer sees between twelve hundred to five thousand messages and views about 15.5 hours of information a day, and this amount is increasing every year. Our business mindsets need to be reengineered to handle this volume of complexity in the same way we do as consumers so that we can support our customers' portfolios along the way.

Marketing and Communications as a Flow

Mihaly Csikszentmihalyi's seminal book, *Flow: The Psychology of Optimal Experience*, talks about methods for managing this constant deluge of tasks, information, and decisions. The act of moving to a more customer-centric approach and understanding how we intercede between those moments needs a more connected process between marketing and communications. Success needs to be orchestrated by a fundamentally different mindset. This needs to be driven by a collaboration-first mindset (and not territorial thinking and behavior). Success must also be focused on the customer's moments and how all forms of marketing (demand, brand, support, thought leadership, crisis management) meet those moments. Leaders need to be constantly curious and open to continual testing and new thinking. Old-world models of singular cause and effect no longer prevail in the digital era.

Sales Are Connected Moments

Recognizing what types of moments matter is a vital skill for a sales leader. We have talked about simple, connected, and sequenced moments starting to prevail in the digital economy. For salespeople to handle this, they have to sense and feel the process a customer is going through and the right moments for interaction. These are classic skills muddied by the enormity of choices available to customers. You can't just be good at recognizing one moment. The skill is to know most if not all of the moments possible for your customers. Again, curiosity and a capacity to know how and when to fail are vital and often unrewarded attributes. High performance in sales, like for athletes, is more about the capacity for risk taking and rapid learning.

Everybody Together All the Time

Information flows 360 degrees in the digital corporation from almost infinite places. We each need to collaborate so we can pass information to and from each other because we all collectively benefit or suffer in the same way. Knowing when and how to share, collaborate, and connect is part of the Digital Helix. This individual and collective responsibility can only be achieved by breaking down traditional and successful boundaries set up in the departmental hierarchy of corporations. Collaboration and sharing require a sense of shared purpose and the capacity to potentially sacrifice our biggest asset, time, for the collective value. We might not be rewarded for it and we may not even understand why we are doing it, but we need confidence and the capacity to push for the greater goal rather than being blindly resolved to failure without a chance to control the result.

In the Moment and One Step Ahead Always

There is a quote that sums up the essence of the book *Flow*: "There are so many moments that we have to divide noise from genuine signal."[2] The world is littered with examples of people not paying attention to these current moments and then not watching or listening to the next piece of evidence that matters. We have talked about the Apple Watch, Uber, and Amazon Web services as examples of digital business models that were ignored in their initial moments because organizations (Swiss watchmakers, taxi companies, and hosting and cloud companies) failed to see the immediate threat and the next steps in their progress. Instead, these companies relied on old-world logic of how to react, rather than using digital to move ahead.

As Dr. Michael Gervais mentioned earlier, winning in business and in sport comes down to a set of key moments. These moments can change in importance for the company or marketplace far faster than ever before. It takes a very different mindset and culture to be present now and also to be a little ahead of that moment. The best athletes have an ability to see things slightly ahead of the curve from the others they play with. It is this capability in business along with the mindset to react that separates the leaders from the losers in any given market.

> "On the job people feel skillful and challenged, and therefore feel more happy, strong, creative, and satisfied. In their free time people feel that there is generally not much to do and their skills are not being used, and therefore they tend to feel more sad, weak, dull, and dissatisfied. Yet they would like to work less and spend more time in leisure.
>
> "What does this contradictory pattern mean? There are several possible explanations, but one conclusion seems inevitable. When it comes to work, people do not heed the evidence of their senses. They disregard the quality of immediate experience, and base their motivation instead on the strongly rooted cultural stereotype of what work is supposed to be like. They think of it as an imposition, a constraint, an infringement of their freedom, and therefore something to be avoided as much as possible."[3]
>
> —**Mihaly Csikszentmihalyi**

None of the concepts in this chapter—risk-taking recovery, a desire of achieving true mastery, and being open to experience the true value of moments—are complex. However, as evidence has shown, it is difficult to achieve them. Having the right mindset to reward and encourage your teams and individuals gives the organization the fuel needed to drive the digital engine to transformation success.

> "When we think of culture and high performance, we focus on assisting people to achieve their greatest potential. The care that it takes and the love that it takes to truly help somebody be their best is a powerful sentiment, and I think it's a motivating, inspiring sentiment when you really mean it and you really act on it. I think the commitment to that is so valuable in terms of leadership, in terms of production for people and so important in creating the environment where people can be their best. That's what the whole effort is about."
> —**Pete Carroll, head coach, Super Bowl Champion Seattle Seahawks**

We are moving to a world where digital will be the norm, and gaining advantage will be critical and difficult once almost everyone is transformed. With that in mind, how will you set your teams up for success and build the right mindsets? When we are all digital, the ability to truly use wearable devices, meditation, and other "personal" tools for business may be one of the few items to separate you from your competitors. Are you ready to compete alongside others who have refocused their organizations on the power of mindset and cultural change and see how far we can all take it?

CHAPTER 16

OVER THE HORIZON TO A BRAVE NEW WORLD, FOR SOME OF US

"My interest is in the future because I am going to spend the rest of my life there."
—Charles F. Kettering

Aldous Huxley and George Orwell each painted somewhat dark views of the future, one dominated by central controls and the other somewhat despairing and inhumane. But the digital future is bright with opportunity. However, this opportunity can also blind some. As digital becomes the preeminent way of business and life, many may make the mistake of ignoring the almost simplistic inevitability of a fully digital world. The UK government's "Digital Inclusion Strategy" policy paper makes an obvious statement that strips away the complexity of experts.

"Being digitally capable can make a significant difference to individuals and organizations day to day. For individuals, this can mean cutting household bills, finding a job, or maintaining contact with distant friends and relatives. For organizations, going online can provide ways to reach more customers and reduce operating costs. The Internet also provides broader benefits by helping to address wider social and economic issues like reducing isolation and supporting economic growth."[1]

Most of the focus of this book has been the journey toward exceptional digital results and helping more enterprises and agencies win and see results. If we assume the future will see both winners and losers, then understanding and getting the future of your organization's role right really matters. Failure to do so might leave you and your teams looking at a digital version of Huxley's or Orwell's view.

Ten Years from Now and a Look at Possible Futures

We believe that key elements of digital will be quite different in ten years. From our conversations with experts across technology, psychology, social, and organizational dynamics, we have identified a core set of principles to frame your future plans. To be clear, we are not trying to predict the future (that is too easy of an exercise and almost always fails the test of time). We are instead trying to lay out some ideas that are going to be key issues and potential challenges going forward. Be advised that some of these might sound strange, but your organization's ability to navigate these potential challenges could well determine the difference between winning and falling behind in the digital future.

Getting Signal-to-Noise Ratios Right Is Critical

In his book *The Power of Noticing*, author Max Bazerman showcases some of the twentieth century's greatest blunders around missed information indicators from the space shuttle *Challenger* disaster to a whole range of financial market misreads and more. The underlying tenent is that in a world of vast chunks, waves, and moments of information, it's vitally important that listeners are able to break through noise and get the right signals. Getting the right message demands, as we have talked about throughout the book, diverse personal and organizational skills (especially the theme and streams portions). With the Internet of Things pumping billions of pieces of data to us all the time, combined with real-time decision-making for suppliers and customers, we are going to have to live in a world with more data (and thus more noise) than ever imagined. Customers will have far more control over what they see, hear, experience, and even feel as they make decisions. They will have virtually instant and comprehensive information on demand via watches and/or smartphones to make decisions. Customers will be able to cut through the noise-to-signal ratios far more easily than a brand can. Imagine a world where the power of knowledge has so severely shifted to consumers that they know maybe 400 percent or 1000 percent more than a brand can ever know in a moment.

Cognizant's research on signal-to-noise ratios, "The Value of Signal (and the Cost of Noise)," illustrates the economics of not getting listening right. In 2016, global IP traffic was 1.1 zettabytes, and this will increase nearly threefold over the next five years. Cognizant's survey says that individuals and groups can make meaning of this with what they term "Meaning Makers." Meaning Makers are able to shift the economic performance of organizations by 11.3 percent in revenue and a reduction of 10.7 percent in costs. Over the next ten years, everything from recruiting based on these new sensing skills to how you enable and empower teams will need to shift to account for and take advantage of this phenomenon. Filtering may well become the number one technical skill while persuading others to listen and act becomes the number two. Together with a keen, almost infant-like curiosity to pursue knowledge, practical insights that change outcomes will largely drive successful individuals and teams to follow the "right" signals and avoid the noise.

In the Future, Everyone Is Simply the Best

In a world dominated by micro markets and even momentary markets of one, you cannot service every segment in every moment. Right now, we are in a mixed world of physical and digital. We might be taking a more aggressive digital lens, but we still live and work in a mostly physical world. Ten to fifteen years from now, that is not likely to be the case. How we communicate, interact, exchange information, and collaborate will change rapidly as the world moves to an all-digital future, enabling every organization to be equal to the best or quite possibly near perfect.

In this digital future, these changes are equally true across the board from organization to employee, organization to customer, organization to supplier, and all other engagements dominated by the digital-first lens. Pareto's law argues that there are a vital few interactions that will matter (the 80:20 rule). These are the key engagements between your best customers and the moments that open up new opportunities and markets. These instants become the vital component for indicating and driving success. While they may change from moment to moment, identification, recognition, and focus in how you market, sell, and manage is vital for sustained victory. Additionally, this keen understanding of the customer will require a new way for organizations to capture more than their fair share, as no one organization can win all the time due to pricing, disloyalty, and even small differences in systems, offerings, and logistics. Constantly asking questions and improving on your organization's "bests" becomes a vital filter for everyday interactions with HR, suppliers, customers, and everyone in between. To be the best an organization can be and improve with every interaction, leaders and teams need to pay vastly more attention to the best 20 percent of your business (customers, suppliers, and employees). You might be able to sell, manage, and service all 100 percent with a digital backbone, but your growth and quality of relationships will be determined by your success with the critical 20 percent first and foremost.

It is an interesting paradox of the digital world that just because you can sell, market, and engage almost at will does not mean that each moment or point of engagement is equally weighted in significance. Take for example the story of Tesco, the premier UK groceries brand for decades. The company was selling 70 percent of the weekly groceries in the UK. Tesco was a brand so dominant it could rightly be called a monopoly. In fact, this almost insurmountable position was backed with leading loyalty programs, incredible advertising, and smart location models. Its success crossed both consumers and investors alike, and even tight shopping hours and missteps like product shortages were tolerated and giggled about because they were somewhat rare and well handled. Even as new brands like Asda, Aldi, and Lidl started or rebirthed as food discounters in the UK, nobody expected them to break Tesco's control, as loyalty data kept showing the same glowing numbers, month in month out.

Two major factors, when combined, were toxic for the brand that was still hanging onto its loyalty data as the indicator of its success.

1. Shopping hours were vastly expanded in the Sunday Trading Act of 1994. There was less pressure for the frantic weekend shopping starting from Thursday and ending in traffic chaos on a Saturday. In addition, online advertising and coupons helped consumers see the value in other offerings as they began to break shopping for the week into chunks.
2. And unlike stores in the French model (Carrefour for example), Tesco was not a superstore that could offer an exponentially higher range of products than the others.

Price equilibriums, geographic choices, wider opening hours, and equal or better logistics from competitors meant that the loyalty card became less and less representative of what was happening or could happen in a changing market. Tesco was looking in the wrong places for data and not focusing on the new 20 percent of their business that mattered. Consumers talked about and easily saw the difference in shopping basket costs between stores in both real life and the media. Additionally, in 2014, expanding even the Sunday shopping hours to twelve hours a day became the new normal for major retailers. Tesco made plenty of other foolish moves, including a US expansion and shifting to a Korean model, in part to try and rebalance the precipitous changes in the UK results. The key failure was relying on an old source of information to try to describe an evolving 20 percent that really mattered to the brand's success. This example clearly shows that being constantly able to push through the information barrier in new ways will be vital for success now and even more so in the all-digital future.

> "There is a risk of information overload that we're trying to manage. There's also an issue of making sure that as we frame reporting and we think about metrics from a digital standpoint, that we educate folks about what we're looking at."
> **—Chris Cox, head of Digital Experience Delivery, USAA**

Marketing a Cyborg Function

In Terry Gilliam's film *Brazil* (1985), the world is dominated by consumerism and really bad delivery, customer service, and attitudes. Even Robert De Niro's portrayal of a revolutionary plumber shows the way that technology (and piping) is so complex as to be unfathomable. As we learn more and get more data, marketing could become that complex as well. In fact, many brands are still adapting and evolving to the new customer-centric world as they change the way they sell, market, communicate, and engage.

Ten years from now, we should and we will be vastly better, if not nearly proficient, across the board. Every marketer and communicator will have the tools and ability to react and deliver more immediately, more predictively, and more automatically. If marketing progresses to a point of near perfect and instant information, then it will likely be dominated by programmable responses to a world driven by consumer needs. Think about it this way, if 80 percent of the moments that matter could be planned with programmed responses and processed with intelligent systems, only asking for human interaction when needed, would we need the vast swathe of marketers we have now for content, pricing, messaging, and other interactions? Once-novel concepts like interactive voice or chat functions are now common components that speed up and automate a vast majority of interactions and needs. From a technology standpoint, not much more needs to happen to continue the automation across more marketing interactions. Once the logic is set, the machines and intelligence could do the rest. From a career and organizational perspective, much of the digital revolution we are all undergoing offers career opportunities, but also career threats.

The Digital Helix and the success with this approach are dominated by the ability to be flexible, collaborate, and use information in near real time to make decisions. This view combined with being responsible to each other and customer experiential portfolios pushes us all on this path. Even if you have not fully embraced the Digital Helix, odds are that your organization marketing and big-data efforts will push you in that direction. What does marketing in your organization look like in ten years with this backdrop?

While we are unlikely to see a Luddite reaction to the revolution in ten years' time, the skills and the actual functions of marketing could be vastly reduced and/or significantly different in nature. For example, marketing may be more about understanding reactions to vast arrays of ongoing tests with a focus on small elements and critical messaging and communications skills. This sets up a need for great communicators with incredible analytic chops or a unique combination of left and right brain skills. With these abilities, marketers will utilize intelligent systems to handle design, delivery, and reactions that can account for and automate 80 percent or more of customers' moments or needs. Like self-driving cars, this feels like the direction we are moving toward, and most believe it is rather inevitable.

We May End Up Job Sharing on Everything

The volume of information, the levels of collaboration required for success, and the complexity of the digital world we live in demands a new way of working. The Digital Helix is the recommended approach because it connects the key components together as an a priori process to be able to handle this speed, complexity, and continual connected fiber of the digital-first organization. If automation of many of the actions and reactions is going to be common in the digital organization, then we need to think about the nature of what employees do as well. As we have already seen, sharing roles are becoming more common and not just for fractional hours. It may sound crazy, but if the systems follow the Digital Helix, they will take more care of themselves, making traditional human guidance less commonplace. This could create pathways to replace functional perspectives and roles with SWAT teams formed and focused on key issues of the moment. In some ways, this world looks at people and marketing in a similar way to how Amazon looks at fulfillment, where automation is the rule, and people are added to the mix when the systems need more of a human touch. We believe that this is certainly one plausible route for marketing over the next ten years. If this comes to pass, what are the implications for career development, job skills, and the physicality of the workspaces?

To highlight these and other possible changes, we interviewed one of the leading futurists in this area, Michael Schrage, research fellow at the MIT Sloan School's Initiative on the Digital Economy.

His views on the future of digital and the work worlds in which they operate provide a radical new lens for not only how to architect for next year but also for the next decade. Rather than chop up the interview into pieces, we thought it would be best for you to see the entire dialogue and context to formulate your own opinions.

Question: What can organizations do to be better prepared for the digital future?

"Clearly, traditional planning models and paradigms don't really work in digital. The ones that do work, embrace some aspect of predictive analytics—they're empirically extrapolating from the statistical past into a probabilistic future.

"If we look at Newell, Simon, and Chase's work on chess with human problem solving from the 1970s, one of the key points is not that chess masters have a superior memory of the pieces on the board, but that they remembered important patterns. Chess masters couldn't recall randomly assorted positions any better than novices could. Grand masters were exceptional at pattern recognition. Experts know there are two kinds of patterns to understand: One is the pattern that you see. These patterns are in front of you and on the board just like in the chess example. These are the patterns that go into your repertoire of responses.

"The other patterns are those you anticipate. Back to the chess example, with these patterns you see the board and the other person's move. Now you know that if they make this move, it's this pattern, or if they make that move, it's that pattern. Recognizing where you are in the moment is different than where you might be next. Experts grasp both.

"This kicks into the challenge of 'combinatorial explosions,' because there are a finite number of patterns people can meaningfully recognize, anticipate, and respond to. If something has happened, you're responding to it. If you anticipate something, though, you will make certain adjustments in anticipation of what you expect.

"When we think ten to fifteen years out about the future of 'pattern recognition,' anticipation and response, we are moving into a cyborg era. The augmentation of people by technology, by choice, or by imposition seems inevitable. I'm not saying everyone will be 'jacked into' their mobile device, but I find it impossible to believe that serious business people won't somehow use some serious technologies to improve their pattern-recognition and decision-making capabilities. People will become 'cyborgs.'

"In this cyborg era, the capacity to manage decisions or design strategy and create plans will be changed forever. What isn't digitally automated will be digitally augmented.

"The past really is prologue: I would argue comfortably that clothes, shoes, and protection were the beginning of augmented people. You are less exposed or you have more flexibility since your feet and your body are protected when you're hunting. The invention of the eyeglasses in the 1500s augmented vision. Attention deficit disorder drugs to give children better ability to concentrate longer are now taken by musicians to be less nervous or more focused on their performances.

"These technologies enhance performance and maybe even change the strategies we use to meet our goals. The role of technology as an augmentation force, both cognitively as well as physically, is going to be the transformation platform for individuals and organizations alike over the next ten years. How people want to become more effective in the productive domains they choose becomes the future narrative.

"It's the top 2 percent in any field that seeks to be at the very, very top and at the same time be seen as someone who transforms their field or their discipline. Think of the world in a new way with high value-adds or high transformatives leading the way. Then, there are those that we can call the competitives, competing in the marketplace against low-cost labor that is competent. The burden is on the individual or organization to decide how they use a digital-first set of ideas and technologies to augment their abilities and move beyond being competent. Also, they will have to identify and understand that some of these technologies are just the cost of entry as we all digitally evolve. Simply put, just as you need a plane or drone to successfully fly today, you will need digital capabilities to successfully think and decide.

"This is the future, and everyone needs to understand that this is how digital and technology will vastly change the landscape and the art of the possible. This is how organizations need to prepare, as missing these manifestations or not anticipating the impact to you and your organization could relegate you to one of the competitives and not high value-adds or high transformatives."

Question: In ten years, how do CEOs need to change or evolve their thinking?

"I am one of those people who does not believe that one can consistently nail market timing. How one does 'risk management' versus 'opportunity assessment' is critical.

"The types of questions the digital CEO should be asking have to change. Time, in a digital world, becomes one of the greatest assets and liabilities. For example, think of a pie chart with two main groupings. The first, as every leader knows, is managing political risk, and there are three questions around this issue: How do you quickly move to digital while managing the political risk, regulatory risk, and legal risk worldwide?

"The second part of the pie chart would be identifying the value-creating community of best employees, customers, and clients. This small group, the 80/20 or the Pareto part of the organization, generates the vast majority of value for the organization.

"For most CEOs, the Paretos should consume between two-thirds to three-quarters of their time. I'd guess the remaining quarter to a third would be a mix of how the CEO believes he or she will improve the median or the Pareto-supporting community.

"These are the things the CEO needs to scour and maintain in order to better support infrastructure for the political and the value-creating needs. In the 80/20 sense, it's the 60 percent of politics and the 40 percent focus on value-creating community that matters. If the CEO has done a less-than-optimal job or less-than-superior job of defining those two communities, he or she will be gone within a very short time. But I freely confess my view is slightly cynical. I feel and fear that politics and the administrative state—not market innovation and individual choice—will cast the larger shadow over executive decision."

It is now time to think about the next ten years in your life. Given these possible shifts and inevitabilities, what changes do you need to start thinking about and looking for to guide your future digital self?

CHAPTER 17

THE NEXT STEPS FOR YOU

"Never look down to test the ground before taking your next step; only he who keeps his eye fixed on the far horizon will find the right road."
—Dag Hammarskjöld

Throughout the book, we have referred to what winners and leaders are doing to get their vital digital transformation efforts to work for them. There is no specific secret vector or set of mapping coordinates to that end game. In fact, there might be tens or even hundreds of pathways to reach the ROI you seek. However, two vital components exist no matter what path you take—the drivers and the challenges. Understanding where your department and/or organization stands against each is vital because it enables you to focus on the nature of the debate and plans around digital transformation. Another critical component is absolute honesty. As any successful organization knows, if you can be brutally honest with where you are and what you have, spending time, effort, and resources on your drivers and challenges sets the stage for the right decisions later on in the process.

"To be successful in any venture, there is a real need to venture into self-discovery. It's really important that the process of self-discovery include everyone across the whole organization. Self-discovery is a fundamental necessity to really be effective. In developing a high-performance culture, you need to respect the uniqueness and the special qualities that people bring in your organization. Self-discovery helps you uncover those qualities so you can bring them to the surface and use them effectively. This is empowering to employees because it shows that you care enough to dig in and to help find their uniqueness. You're validating them and also celebrating these qualities. This style becomes a really crucial strength of the makeup of your organization. Plus, you can demonstrate that you really do care and that you are sincere about trying to find where people can be positioned and postured at their very best."
—**Pete Carroll, head coach, Super Bowl Champion Seattle Seahawks**

In terms of the actions taken, it is easy to get paralyzed with the complexity of the tasks at hand. As a part of this, you cannot set high expectations or hope that every one of the seven Digital Helix components will immediately deliver or produce results consistently. As we have discussed at length, there are a few absolutes to keep in mind:

1. Deep and ongoing executive engagement is vital to ensure that both the current and future plans are being guided from a holistic perspective.
2. Changing the way we architect, manage, and use information in faster time frames is crucial.
3. Thinking about strategy in a different, post–Michael Porter Five Forces world is critical and can be the key to winning or losing.

The seven components of the Digital Helix are the foundation to successful digital transformations, and they all have important roles to play in the rebuilding of your corporation with digital DNA at its center. But as we have mentioned, success requires that each and every component work together in a highly interconnected way. To get these critical components in sync, finding the first few simple stepping-stones is important. Our original research with the Economist Intelligence Unit in 2012 showed some of the early signals for both successes and failures. Organizations that neither committed fully nor prepared to handle the future of the digital-first organization often failed, and the setbacks impacted far more than just ROI. These signals were further illustrated by the second and larger round of research we conducted in 2013. When looking at more than a thousand case studies, we could clearly recognize the early patterns for success. Many brands and government entities recognized the value and economics of digital, but only a fraction fully understood the path and fortitude required.

Every leader we have interviewed, researched, or received data from says the energy for digital transformation is here inside every organization. The secret is to balance the importance of the seven components and to plot the right course. You can plot for yourself all the possible areas where one or more of the components work well together. These areas could include: executives as explorers, theme and stream listening, sales as connected moments, and marketing and communications as a flow. But remember, brutal honestly is required throughout the process. Giving the organization credit for something they don't deserve or cannot achieve is pointless.

Real effort and coordination are required to bring the other components into alignment using one step ahead and with everybody being responsible for each other. As we have seen in many instances, this leads to great initial momentum for the organization, but a sudden change in market conditions or competitive landscape stalls longer-term success and isolates digital transformation and the benefits to a few areas. Just one misaligned or inactive component can be the difference between digital success and falling behind the competition.

As discussed, the right construction process is critical. Not only do you have to ask yourself tough questions inside each of the seven barriers and Seven Challenges, but you will need to constantly question the performance and dynamics inside each of the seven Digital Helix components. Self-awareness, or the lack thereof, is about 50 percent of the challenge organizations face. None of this is easy. Trying to convert the organization and their daily processes to the new world of the digital-first organization is incredibly tough. Fortunately, it can be done, and we are confident that the tools, frameworks, and insights in this book will give you the ability to succeed. In fact, you probably bought the book because you are either trying to implement digital right now, or have had less than stellar results in the past. Either way, you are now well armed to understand the mistakes made or that could be made along the way and how to overcome the hurdles you may face. You are prepared, headed in the right direction, and ready for the challenge. You are already way ahead of the competition because you read this book.

Now is the time to ask the question: What is your potential first hundred-day plan for becoming a digital leader?

We wish you the best of luck!

AFTERWORD

As the IP for this area evolves, we will continue to publish addendums, examples, and tools for you to use in your own digital transformation journeys. We have an app to use that will have the core frameworks, questions, and tools that the book is based on, giving you the ability to tap back into the ideas, best practices, and social feedback from other practitioners as you go.

The process of researching, learning, and writing this book was a wonderful experience. Everybody we interviewed was especially forthright and honest about their ideas, practices, and experiences and generously shared their insights and time. Tapping into the collective learnings and ideas from these thirty or more digital leaders via extensive interviews taught us far more than we could have hoped for and helped us sculpt and validate the ideas in the book. We were also fortunate to have the collective support of our former colleagues at ICF, and we are grateful. ICF has been an amazing place to see these ideas bloom and come to fruition.

ACKNOWLEDGMENTS

To the two most important people to us, Lara Gale and Wendi Aarons, we feel a thank you is not enough. For each of us, you are the compasses that we navigate with and the very joy of each of our days. Your guidance, humor, and candor as we went through the whole process of the book is more valuable than we could ever account for, and allowing us to invest the time and energy in such a focused way is a gift we will be ever grateful for. This book is dedicated to you both. To Georgia, Aramis, and Tennyson, Jack, Sam, and Teddy, we look forward to many more days playing in the sun together.

NOTES

Introduction

1. "The 2016 State of Digital Transformation," Brian Solis et al., Altimeter@ Prophet, September 2016, http://www2.prophet.com/The-2016-State-of-Digital-Transformation.

Chapter 1

1. "The 2016 State of Digital Transformation," Brian Solis et al., Altimeter@ Prophet, September 2016, http://www2.prophet.com/The-2016-State-of-Digital-Transformation.
2. Jim C. Collins, *Good to Great: Why Some Companies Make the Leap... and Others Don't* (New York: William Collins, 2001), 10.

Chapter 2

1. Eric Hobsbawm, *The Age of Revolution: 1789–1848* (New York: Vintage; 1st Vintage Books, 1996), 52.
2. "Digital Recruitment: A New Era of Job Seeking," John Brasington, Recruiting Blogs, August 31, 2014, http://www.recruitingblogs.com/profiles/blogs/digital-recruitment-a-new-era-of-job-seeking.
3. "51% of U.S. Adults Bank Online," Susannah Fox, PewResearchCenter, August 7, 2013, http://www.pewinternet.org/2013/08/07/51-of-u-s-adults-bank-online/.
4. "Business Communications Never Sleep in 2015," Evie Goldstein, RingCentral Blog, December 19, 2014, https://www.ringcentral.com/blog/2014/12/business-communications-never-sleep-2015/.
5. "Social Networks: Are They Eroding Our Social Lives?" Sam Laird, Mashable, April 25, 2012, http://mashable.com/2012/04/25/social-networks-study/#NFhLmYEvT5kz.
6. "70+ Digital Transformation Statistics," SantokuPartners, December 11, 2013, http://www.slideshare.net/SantokuPartners/70-digital-transformation-statistics.
7. "Percentage of Disposable Income Spent Online in Selected Countries," Statista,

February 2012, https://www.statista.com/statistics/227397/share-of-dispsable-income-spent-online-in-selected-countries/.

8. "The Salesman Who Doesn't Sell," Corey Dahl, LifeHealthPro, December 18, 2015, http://www.lifehealthpro.com/2015/12/18/the-salesman-who-doesnt-sell?page_all=1&slreturn=1477511943.
9. "Winning the Digital Game with a Human Touch," Sanjay Dawar et al., Accenture, October 2016, https://www.accenture.com/in-en/insight-global-consumer-pulse-research-india.
10. "15 Social Media Statistics That Every Business Needs to Know," Erin Richards-Kunkel, Business2Community, February 26, 2013, http://www.business2community.com/social-media/15-social-media-statistics-that-every-business-needs-to-know-0418173.
11. "Gartner Predicts That Refusing to Communicate by Social Media Will Be as Harmful to Companies as Ignoring Phone Calls or Emails Is Today," Gartner, August 1, 2012, http://www.gartner.com/newsroom/id/2101515.
12. "10 Customer Service Stats and What They Mean for Your Contact Center," Tim Pickard, Salesforce, January 14, 2015, https://www.salesforce.com/blog/2015/01/ten-customer-service-stats-what-they-mean-your-contact-center-gp.html.
13. "5 Tips for Providing Personalized Customer Service in the Digital Age," Melissa Thompson, CustomerThink, April 21, 2015, http://customerthink.com/5-tips-for-providing-personalized-customer-service-in-the-digital-age/.
14. "U.S. Smartphone Use in 2015," Aaron Smith, PewResearchCenter, April 1, 2015, http://www.pewinternet.org/2015/04/01/us-smartphone-use-in-2015/.
15. "Cisco Visual Networking Index: Global Mobile Data Traffic Forecast Update, 2016–2021 White Paper," Cisco, February 7, 2017, http://www.cisco.com/c/en/us/solutions/collateral/service-provider/visual-networking-index-vni/white_paper_c11-520862.html.
16. "70+ Digital Transformation Statistics," SantokuPartners, December 11, 2013, http://www.slideshare.net/SantokuPartners/70-digital-transformation-statistics.
17. "10 Global Communication Trends in 2014," Jeremy Galbraith, WPP, March 2014, http://www.wpp.com/wpp/marketing/publicrelations/10-global-communication-trends-2014/.
18. "How Fitbit Is Cashing in on the High-Tech Fitness Trend," Jennifer Wang, Entrepreneur, July 28, 2012, http://www.entrepreneur.com/article/223780.
19. "70+ Digital Transformation Statistics," SantokuPartners, December 11, 2013, http://www.slideshare.net/SantokuPartners/70-digital-transformation-statistics.
20. "Thanks Social Media—Our Average Attention Span Is Now Shorter Than Goldfish," Michael Brenner, Marketing Insider Group, May 19, 2014, http://www.b2bmarketinginsider.com/content-marketing/thanks-social-media-average-attention-span-now-shorter-goldfish.
21. "100 Amazing Google Search Statistics and Fun Facts," Craig Smith, DMR, March 15, 2017, http://expandedramblings.com/index.php/by-the-numbers-a-gigantic-list-of-google-stats-and-facts/2/.

22. "Google Search Statistics," Internet Live Stats, accessed March 30, 2017, http://www.internetlivestats.com/google-search-statistics/.
23. "160 Amazing YouTube Statistics," Craig Smith, DMR, March 2017, http://expandedramblings.com/index.php/youtube-statistics/.
24. "15 Social Media Statistics That Every Business Needs to Know," Erin Richards-Kunkel, Business2Community, February 26, 2013, http://www.business2community.com/social-media/15-social-media-statistics-that-every-business-needs-to-know-0418173.
25. "Cutting Down On Choice Is The Best Way To Make Better Decisions," Carolyn Cutrone, Business Insider, January 10, 2013, http://www.businessinsider.com/too-many-choices-are-bad-for-business-2012-12?op=1.
26. "The Myth of 5,000 Ads," J. Walker Smith, Yankelovich, accessed March 30, 2017, http://cbi.hhcc.com/writing/the-myth-of-5000- ads/.
27. "What to Do When There Are Too Many Product Choices on the Store Shelves? Learn How to Navigate the Flood of Options—and Save Money," Consumer Reports, January 2014, http://www.consumerreports.org/cro/magazine/2014/03/too-many-product-choices-in-supermarkets/index.htm.
28. Peter Drucker, quoted in Philip Kotler, *Standing Room Only: Strategies for Marketing the Performing Arts* (Cambridge: Harvard Business Review Press, 1997), 33.
29. "Silicon Valley Self-Driving Car Startup's Value Hits $1.55B," Cromwell Schubarth, Silicon Valley Business Journal, November 7, 2016, http://www.bizjournals.com/sanjose/news/2016/11/07/silicon-valley-self-driving-car-startups-value.html.

Chapter 3

1. John Maynard Keynes, *The General Theory of Employment, Interest and Money* (London: Macmillan, 1936), 3.
2. Peter Drucker, *Innovation and Entrepreneurship* (New York: HarperBusiness; Reprint edition, 2006).
3. "Digital Transformation, Part 6: Examples of Digital Transformation Done Right," Sven Denecken, ZDNet, October 24, 2014, http://www.zdnet.com/article/digital-transformation-part-6-examples-of-digital-transformation-done-right/.
4. "75 Customer Service Facts, Quotes & Statistics," Help Scout, accessed March 30, 2017, https://www.helpscout.net/75-customer-service-facts-quotes-statistics/.
5. "Why You Can't Ignore Millennials," Dan Schawbel, *Forbes*, September 4, 2013, http://www.forbes.com/sites/danschawbel/2013/09/04/why-you-cant-ignore-millennials/#7b2f4b2f6c65.
6. "The Deloitte Millennial Survey 2017," Deloitte, accessed March 30, 2017, https://www2.deloitte.com/global/en/pages/about-deloitte/articles/millennialsurvey.html.
7. "The Kauffman Index Startup Activity 2015," Robert W. Fairlie et al., Kauffman Foundation, June 2015, http://www.kauffman.org/~/media/kauffman_org/research%20reports%20and%20covers/2015/05/kauffman_index_startup_activity_national_trends_2015.pdf.

8. "Mobile Check Deposits Continue to Rise," John Ginovsky, Banking Exchange, September 3, 2015, http://www.bankingexchange.com/news-feed/item/5716-mobile-check-deposits-continue-to-rise.

9. "10 Trends for 2015 Report," Trendwatching, November 2014, http://trendwatching.com/trends/10-trends-for-2015/.

10. "The Future Has Arrived—It's Just Not Evenly Distributed Yet," Quote Investigator, accessed March 30, 2017, http://quoteinvestigator.com/2012/01/24/future-has-arrived/.

11. "Negative Reviews—A Golden Opportunity for Business," Better Business Bureau, September 15, 2014, https://www.bbb.org/phoenix/news-events/business-tips/2014/09/negative-reviews-a-golden-opportunity-for-business/.

12. "75 Customer Service Facts, Quotes & Statistics," Help Scout, accessed March 30, 2017, https://www.helpscout.net/75-customer-service-facts-quotes-statistics/.

13. "75 Customer Service Facts, Quotes & Statistics," Help Scout, accessed March 30, 2017, https://www.helpscout.net/75-customer-service-facts-quotes-statistics/.

14. "Online Product Research," Jim Jansen, PewResearchCenter, September 29, 2010, http://www.pewinternet.org/2010/09/29/online-product-research/.

15. "11 of the 12 Best Global Brands Use Creative Crowdsourcing," Yannig Roth, YannigRoth.com, March 23, 2012, https://yannigroth.com/2012/03/23/xx-of-the-100-best-global-brands-use-creative-crowdsourcing/.

16. "Satya Nadella email to employees on first day as CEO," Satya Nadella, Microsoft, February 4, 2014, https://news.microsoft.com/2014/02/04/satya-nadella-email-to-employees-on-first-day-as-ceo/#sm.000q7i3em6igf2811nz2buq1b8iq8#BCoFCqRPDeDQoqTd.97.

17. "How Adaptive Sourcing Helps CIOs Revolutionize Innovative IT Sourcing," Ben Kerschberg, *Forbes*, August 7, 2014, http://www.forbes.com/sites/benkerschberg/2014/08/07/how-adaptive-sourcing-helps-cios-revolutionize-innovative-it-sourcing/#4efaf2c72e27.

18. "The Brilliant Invention That's Setting an Indiegogo Record Is Something You'd Never Expect," NextShark, March 9, 2015, http://nextshark.com/the-brilliant-invention-thats-setting-a-5-million-indiegogo-record-is-something-youd-never-expect/.

19. "Industrialized Crowdsourcing," Marcus Shingles and Jonathan Trichel, Deloitte, February 21, 2014, https://dupress.deloitte.com/dup-us-en/focus/tech-trends/2014/2014-tech-trends-crowdsourcing.html.

20. "Business Lessons from American Express CEO Ken Chenault," Zach Bulygo, KISSmetrics, May 24, 2013, https://blog.kissmetrics.com/lessons-from-ken-chenault/.

21. "How Much Money Does a New Startup Need," Stuart Ellman, Business Insider, September 26, 2013, http://www.businessinsider.com/how-much-money-does-a-new-startup-need-2013-9.

22. GoFundMe, accessed March 30, 2017, http://www.crowdfunding.com/.

23. "Why Businesses Succeed and Fail," Alyson Shontell, Entrepreneur, January 12, 2011, https://www.entrepreneur.com/article/217843.

24. "25+ Mind Blowing Stats About Business Today—Ctrl Alt Delete," Mitch Joel, May 26, 2013, http://www.slideshare.net/mitchjoel/ctrl-alt-delete-slideshare-21954452.

25. "Kickstarter Statistics Dissected," Maxim Wheatley, Alley Watch, July 31, 2013, http://www.alleywatch.com/2013/07/kickstarter-statistics-dissected/.

26. "By the Numbers: What Are the Key Ingredients of Startup Success?" Murray Goldstein, Blue, accessed March 30, 2017, http://www.coxblue.com/numbers-key-ingredients-startup-success/.

27. "29 Quotes on the Future of Business," Michael Brenner, Digitalist Magazine, August 30, 2013, http://www.digitalistmag.com/innovation/2013/08/30/29-quotes-on-the-future-of-business-0466930.

28. "Who Art Thou, Chief Digital Officer?" Bryan Kirschner, Entrepreneur, February 13, 2014, https://www.entrepreneur.com/article/231484.

29. Mitch Joel, *Ctrl Alt Delete* (New York: Grand Central Publishing, 2013).

30. The quotation is attributed to Welch among public figures and in online sources such as Goodreads.

31. "Keynote Feedback: Some Mind-Blowing Stats," Jim Carroll, JimCarroll.com, September 2011, https://www.jimcarroll.com/2011/10/keynote-feedback-some-mind-blowing-stats/.

32. Ibid.

33. "99 Amazing Facts on the Future of Business," *Forbes*, October 8, 2013, http://www.forbes.com/sites/sap/2013/10/08/99-amazing-facts-on-the-future-of-business/#41849e101c06.

34. "Why 'Big Data' Is a Big Deal," Jonathan Shaw, *Harvard Magazine*, March 2014, http://harvardmagazine.com/2014/03/why-big-data-is-a-big-deal.

35. "3 out of 4 Brands Could Disappear and Most People Wouldn't Care," Susan Gunelius, Corporate Eye, June 19, 2013, http://www.corporate-eye.com/main/3-out-of-4-brands-could-disappear-and-most-people-wouldnt-care/.

36. "99 Fact on the Future Of Business," SAP, October 3, 2013, http://www.slideshare.net/sap/99-facts-on-the-future-of-business.

37. Clayton Christensen, *The Innovator's Dilemma: When New Technologies Cause Great Firms to Fail* (Cambridge, MA: Harvard Business Review Press; 1st edition, 1997).

38. "The Digital Advantage: How Digital Leaders Outperform Their Peers in Every Industry," George Westerman et al., CapGemini, https://www.capgemini.com/resource-file-access/resource/pdf/The_Digital_Advantage__How_Digital_Leaders_Outperform_their_Peers_in_Every_Industry.pdf..

Chapter 4

1. Fritjof Capra, *Tao of Physics: An Exploration of the Parallels Between Modern Physics and Eastern Mysticism* (Boulder, Colorado: Shambhala, fifth edition, 2010), 68.

2. "How to Beat the Transformation Odds," David Jacquemont et al, McKinsey Consulting, April 2015, http://www.mckinsey.com/business-functions/organization/our-insights/how-to-beat-the-transformation-odds.

Chapter 5

1. "Digital Transformation and the Race Against Digital Darwinism," Brian Solis, BrianSolis.com, September 9, 2014, http://www.briansolis.com/2014/09/digital-transformation-race-digital-darwinism/.
2. "An Interview with Angela Ahrendts," Didier Bonnet, CapGemini, 2012, https://www.capgemini.com/resource-file-access/resource/pdf/DIGITAL_LEADERSHIP__An_interview_with_Angela_Ahrendts.pdf.
3. Ibid.
4. "Discussions on Digital: How Large and Small Companies Build a Digital Culture," Brian Gregg, McKinsey, October 2016, http://www.mckinsey.com/business-functions/digital-mckinsey/our-insights/discussions-on-digital-how-large-and-small-companies-build-a-digital-culture.
5. "Customer Experience: At SanDisk It Is the Bottom Line," Michael Connor, Insanely Great, June 9, 2014, http://www.creatinginsanelygreat.com/sandisk-case-study-2/.
6. "Harnessing the 'Bang' Stories from the Frontline," Deloitte, 2014, https://www2.deloitte.com/content/dam/Deloitte/au/Documents/Building%20Lucky%20Country/Deloitte_au_technology_digital_disruption_harnessing_the_bang_2014.pdf.
7. Ibid.
8. "In Focus: Lou Gerstner," CNN.com, World Business, Global Office, July 2, 2004, http://edition.cnn.com/2004/BUSINESS/07/02/gerstner.interview/.
9. Charles G. Sieloff, "If Only HP Knew What HP Knows: the Roots of Knowledge Management at Hewlett-Packard," *Journal of Knowledge Management* 3, no. 1 (1999): 47–53, http://www.emeraldinsight.com/doi/abs/10.1108/13673279910259385.
10. "Why Strategy Execution Unravels and What to Do About It," Donald Sull, Rebecca Homkes, and Charles Sull, *Harvard Business Review,* March 2015, https://hbr.org/2015/03/why-strategy-execution-unravelsand-what-to-do-about-it.
11. "Google Reveals Its 9 Principles of Innovation," Kathy Chin Leong, FastCompany, November 20, 2013, https://www.fastcompany.com/3021956/how-to-be-a-success-at-everything/googles-nine-principles-of-innovation.
12. "5 Best Practices for Developing IoT Applications with Rapid Experimentation," Johan den Haan, The Internet Of Things, March 11, 2017, http://www.theinternetofthings.eu/johan-den-haan-5-best-practices-developing-iot-applications-rapid-experimentation.
13. "Embracing Digital Technology," Michael Fitzgerald, Nina Kruschwitz, Didier Bonnet, and Michael Welch, MIT Sloan Review, October 07, 2013, http://sloanreview.mit.edu/projects/embracing-digital-technology/.
14. "Michael E. Porter on Why Companies Must Address Social Issues," Dan Schawbel, Forbes.com, October 9, 2012, https://www.forbes.com/sites/danschawbel/2012/10/09/michael-e-porter-on-why-companies-must-address-social-issues/#831c4a4468ae.

Chapter 6

1. The quotation is attributed to Fuller among public figures and in online sources such as Goodreads.

Chapter 7

1. PulsePoint Group and the Economist Intelligence Unit: Economics of the Socially Engaged Enterprise 2012 and 2013.

Chapter 8

1. "5 Time-Tested Success Tips from Amazon Founder Jeff Bezos," John Greathouse, *Forbes,* April 30, 2013, https://www.forbes.com/sites/johngreathouse/2013/04/30/5-time-tested-success-tips-from-amazon-founder-jeff-bezos/#5d0d08bd370c.
2. "Becoming a First-Class Noticer," Max H. Bazerman, *Harvard Business Review*, August 16, 2014, https://hbr.org/2014/07/becoming-a-first-class-noticer.
3. Daniel Kahneman, *Thinking, Fast and Slow* (New York: Farrar, Straus and Giroux; 2011), 218.
4. China Miéville, *Embassytown* (New York: Del Rey Books, 2012), 345.
5. "The New 21st Century Leaders," Bill George, *Harvard Business Review*, April 30, 2010, https://hbr.org/2010/04/the-new-21st-century-leaders-1.html.

Chapter 10

1. "How Yelp Can Help Your Small Business," Cayan Insights, Cayan, September 2, 2013, https://cayan.com/how-yelp-can-help-your-business.
2. Ibid.

Chapter 11

1. "Big Business Beyond the Beach Holiday," BBC.com, July 22, 2016, http://www.bbc.com/news/world-us-canada-36870975.

Chapter 13

1. "Embracing Agile," Darrell K. Rigby, Jeff Sutherland, and Hirotaka Takeuchi, *Harvard Business Review*, May 2016, https://hbr.org/2016/05/embracing-agile.
2. "Leadership Principles," Amazon, https://www.amazon.jobs/en/principles.
3. "Our Leadership Principles," Amazon, https://www.amazon.com/p/feature/p34qgjcv93n37yd.
4. "12 Business Lessons You Can Learn from Amazon Founder and CEO Jeff Bezos," Zach Bulygo, KISSmetrics, January 19, 2013, https://blog.kissmetrics.com/lessons-from-jeff-bezos/.

5. "Why Leadership Training Fails—and What to Do About It," Michael Beer, Magnus Finnström, and Derek Schrader, *Harvard Business Review*, October 2016, https://hbr.org/2016/10/why-leadership-training-fails-and-what-to-do-about-it.

"The Performance Management Revolution," Peter Cappelli and Anna Tavis, *Harvard Business Review*, October 2016, https://hbr.org/2016/10/the-performance-management-revolution.

"AT&T's Talent Overhaul," John Donovan and Cathy Benko, *Harvard Business Review*, October 2016, https://hbr.org/2016/10/atts-talent-overhaul.

Chapter 14

1. "Why Strategy Execution Unravels and What to Do About It," Donald Sull, Rebecca Homkes, and Charles Sull, *Harvard Business Review*, March 2015, https://hbr.org/2015/03/why-strategy-execution-unravelsand-what-to-do-about-it.

2. Ibid.

3. "Discussions on Digital: How Large and Small Companies Build a Digital Culture," Brian Gregg, McKinsey, http://www.mckinsey.com/business-functions/digital-mckinsey/our-insights/discussions-on-digital-how-large-and-small-companies-build-a-digital-culture.

4. "12 Business Lessons You Can Learn from Amazon Founder and CEO Jeff Bezos," Zach Bulygo, KISSmetrics, January 19, 2013, https://blog.kissmetrics.com/lessons-from-jeff-bezos/.

5. Ibid.

Chapter 15

1. "As Mark Zuckerberg Turns 30, His 10 Best Quotes as CEO," Jason Fell, *Entrepreneur*, May 14, 2014, https://www.entrepreneur.com/article/233890.

2. Mihaly Csikszentmihalyi, *Flow: The Psychology of Optimal Experience* (New York: Harper & Row, 1990).

3. Ibid.

Chapter 16

1. "Digital Inclusion and Government Services," Becca Russell et al., Digital Inclusion Strategy, UK, November 21, 2014, https://digitalinclusion.blog.gov.uk/2014/11/21/digital-inclusion-and-government-services/.

INDEX

A

Adidas, 36
AfriGal Tech, 11–12
The Age of Revolution (Hobsbawm), 18
Agile development model, 173–74
agility, 144, 183–85
Ahrendts, Angela, 67–68
"The AI Revolution" (Urban), xi
Aldi, 212
"all for one and one for all" component, 109, 111, 171–82
    aligning teams with digital goals, 172–73
    Amazon's leadership principles, 175–78
    binding mechanism and enabling structure, 178
    essential nature of, 171–74
    hiring, coaching, and talent development, 180
    inspiring unity, 175
    makeshift workarounds, 173
    mindset and cultural development, 206
    relationship to other Digital Helix components, 144–45, 179, 181, 191
    support and trust, 174
Allstate, 160
All the President's Men (film), 85
"all together and one step ahead" component, 109, 112, 183–93
    advocacy and support system, 187
    agility, 183–85
    balance between strategists and executors, 192
    combining strategies, 190
    elements of alternative strategy development, 185–86
    extensive experimentation, 186
    infinite scalability, 189
    metrics, 189
    mindset and cultural development, 207
    no single perfect strategy, 184–85
    play-it-safe behavior, 183
    relationship to other Digital Helix components, 145, 190–91
Ally, 160, 162
Altimeter, 56
Amazon, ix, 35, 105, 138, 181, 215
    Amazon Machine Learning, 11
    Amazon Web Services, 25, 36, 207
    "Dash" devices, 188
    leadership principles, 175–78
    "pioneer spirit," 179
    Prime, 189
    shipping, 187–89
American Airlines, 45
Andretti, Mario, 113
Android, 84, 144
Appirio/Topcoder, 40
Apple, 23, 35, 43, 67, 80, 144, 180, 207
Asda, 212
Audi, 188
augmented people, 217
"authentic experience," 157
Azure cloud, x

B

Backman, Paul, 37
"backward compatibility" thinking, 91
Bailey, Christopher, 68
banking, 22, 37, 160
Barbin, Chris, 39
Barr, Jud, 19, 186
Bazerman, Max H., 115, 210
Best Buy, 72–73
Bezos, Jeff, 42, 113, 178–79, 188
Bing, 129
Blockbuster, 81
Blogger, 83
Bray, David, 107, 133
Brazil (film), 214
Burberry, 67–68
Business Insider, 41

C

Cap Gemini, 46
Capitalism, Socialism and Democracy (Schumpeter), xii
Capra, Fritjof, 51–52
Carrefour, 213
Carroll, Pete, 5, 56–57, 196–97, 208, 220
Cars.com, 138
"Challenger" sales model, 170
The Challenger Sale: Taking Control of the Customer Conversation (Dixon and Adamson), 170
Chambers, John, x
change. *See also* digital transformation
    adjusting and adapting to, 21, 125–26
    for CEOs in next ten years, 218
    exponential rate of, 42–45
    scale of digital change, 22–24
    small changes and long-term results, 92, 96–98
    Trend Spotting and Tracking Template, 44–45
Charif, Mona, 19–20
Chase, William G., 216
Chatman, Reginald, 74–75
Chenault, Ken, 40
chess masters, 214–15
Christensen, Clayton, 45
Churchill, Winston, 183
Cisco, x

Citi, 142–43
Cognizant, 211
Colella, Vanessa, 120, 134, 142–43, 153
Colgate, 25–26
Collins, Jim, 15–16
Cook, James, 121
Cox, Chris, 10, 93, 126–27, 131, 151, 156, 160–61, 213
Crawford, Colin, 180, 191–92
creative destruction, xii
Creators, 60–61
Crest, 25–26
Crick, Francis, xii, 105
CRM (customer relationship management), 68–69
crowdfunding, 41
crowdsourcing, 38, 40, 46
Csikszentmihalyi, Mihaly, 205, 207
cultural development. *See* mindset and cultural development
customer abandonment, 35, 55, 73, 162
customer service feedback, 35, 38, 142
"customers' experiential portfolios" component, 109–11, 137–47
    Catherine wheel diagram, 140–41
    identifying and handling experiences within, 139–40
    interconnectivity of experiences, 138–39
    leveraging, 138–39
    measuring value or effect of, 145–46
    mindset and cultural development, 205
    relationship to other Digital Helix components, 140–45, 191
customization, 18–19, 24–26, 36
CVS, 129
cyborg era, 216–17

D

Darwin, Charles, 21
Deloitte, 56
De Niro, Robert, 214
DHL, 188
"The Digital Advantage: How Digital Leaders Outperform Their Peers in Every Industry" (Cap Gemini/MIT), 46
digital-first perspective, xii, 22, 34, 87, 105, 111

Digital Helix framework, xii, 1, 3, 16, 108, 220–21
   "all for one and one for all" component, 109, 111, 171–82
   "all together and one step ahead" component, 109, 112, 183–93
   "customers' experiential portfolios" component, 109–11, 137–47
   "executives as explorers" component, 108–10, 113–24
   future of digital transformation, 214–15
   "marketing and communications as flow" component, 109, 111, 149–57
   overview of, 3
   "sales as connected moments" component, 109, 111, 159–70
   "themes and streams" component, 109–10, 125–36
"Digital Inclusion Strategy" policy paper (UK), 209–10
digital revolution, xi, 11–12
   mass customization, 18–19
   scale and rate of change, 22–24
   "seven pressures" (Drucker), 32–33
digital transformation, 1–2
   absolutes, 220
   adjusting and adapting to change, 21
   affinity with, 91
   attempts that miss the mark, 9–10, 12, 19–21
   changes wrought by, 11–12
   concerns of CEOs regarding, xi
   creative destruction, xii
   digital wrapping trap, 14–15
   enabling customer success, 24–26
   exponential change, x–xi
   framing debate regarding, 89–90
   future of, 209–18
   gravitation toward new concepts, 91–96
   "greater than the sum of their parts" viewpoint, 13–16
   investing in isolation, 13–14
   key conceptual shifts, 93–96
   leadership and, ix–x
   learning from failures, 58–59, 84–85
   mass customization, 18–19
   momentum led by successes, 92, 101–2
   myths and realities of, 46–47
   need for framework and strategy, 13–14, 16, 20–21
   resistance to, 10
   small changes, 92, 96–98
   technological change versus, viii, 26
   time investment in, 89–90, 98–101
   transition between third and fourth industrial revolutions, xi
   vital components of, 219
Digital Transformation Reality Check, 47
The Double Helix (Watson), xii
Dreamers, 60–61
Drucker, Peter, 25, 32–33, 161

E

eBay, 35–36
Ecolab, 14
e-commerce, 22–23
Economist Intelligence Unit, 12, 52, 221
Edison, Thomas. A., 58
80:20 rule (Pareto's law), 212–13, 218
Einstein, Albert, 89
Eloqua, 81, 85
Embassytown (Miéville), 117
"Embracing Agile, How to Master the Process That Is Transforming Management" (Rigby, Sutherland, and Takeuchi), 173–74
Escape Velocity (Moore), 31
"everyone together all the time" component. *See* "all for one and one for all" component
"executives as explorers" component, 108–10, 113–24
   accepting risk in information and enablement, 121–22
   actions versus mandates, 122
   enabling, embracing, then mandating, 118–19
   expansion of information, 114–15
   experimentation, 120–22
   focus on information driving transformation, 114–16
   letting go and seeking, 120
   mindset and cultural development, 204

motivated blindness, 115
questionnaire/audit regarding, 122–23
realigning and rehiring, 119
relationship to other Digital Helix components, 156, 181, 190–91
valuing journey and path, 117–18
What You See Is All There Is, 115–16
experiential portfolios. *See* "customers' experiential portfolios" component

F

Facebook, 105
failure
    failing well, 83
    learning from, 28, 58–59, 84–85, 186–87, 204
    propensity for handling, 199
    taking risk and failure hand in hand, 203
Faley, Kelly, 145
fashion industry, 18–19
FedEx, 188
filtering. *See* signal-to-noise ratios and filtering
Flip, x
flow. *See* "marketing and communications as flow" component
Flow Hive, 40
Flow: The Psychology of Optimal Experience (Csikszentmihalyi), 205, 207
Forbes Insights, xi
Forbes Media, ix
Ford, Henry, 51
Fuller, Buckminster, 89–90

G

Gartner, 39
Gen X, 162
Gen Y, 42
Gerstner, Lou, 78
Gervais, Michael, 85–86, 98, 119, 190, 197–203, 207
Gibson, William, 38
Gilliam, Terry, 214
Gladwell, Malcolm, 171
Glassdoor, 37
GM, ix, 181
Gmail, 84

Godbout, Greg, 92
GoFundMe, 41
Goldcorp, 40
Good to Great: Why Some Companies Make the Leap...and Others Don't (Collins), 15–16
Google, 23, 80, 82–84, 105, 144, 163, 186–87
"greater than the sum of their parts" viewpoint, 13–16, 76, 114, 122, 135
green revolution, 14
"green-washing," 14
Groupon, 80

H

Hallmark, 131–32, 135–36
Hammarskjöld, Dag, 219
Harvard Business Review (HBR), 173–74
Harvard University, 42
healthcare.gov, 70–71
Hendrix, Jimi, 137
Hobsbawm, Eric, 17–18
Holacracy, 41
Holgate, Rick, 174–75
Homkes, Rebecca, 80, 184
HP, 79
Huxley, Aldous, 209

I

IBM, 132, 160, 167
Impossible Foods, 185
Incrementalists, 60–61
Industrial Revolution, 9–10, 17–18, 21
infographics, 163
Innovation and Entrepreneurship (Drucker), 32
The Innovator's Dilemma (Christensen), 45
The Innovator's Hypothesis (Schrage), 2
An Inquiry into the Nature and Causes of the Wealth of Nations (Smith), 11, 197
Instagram, 23
insurance, 23, 36, 70–71
Interbrand, 38, 146
Internet of Things (IoT), 18, 74
"in the moment and one step ahead always" component. *See* "all together and one step ahead" component
Iwata, Jon, 4, 21, 132, 167, 173–74

J

Jacquemont, David, 58
job applications, 22
Jobs, Steve, 144
JTB Consulting, 19

K

Kahnemen, Daniel, 115–16
Kardgaard, Rich, xi–xii
Kauffman Firm Survey, 37
Kentley-Klay, Tim, 27
Kettering, Charles F., 207
Keynes, John Maynard, 32
Kickstarter, 41–42
Kierkegaard, Søren, 159
Kodak, 81
Kostin, Gwynne, 91
Kurzweil, Ray, xi

L

Lamoureux, Kristin, 157
Lao Tzu, 149
Lasik, 163
Lee, David, 72–73, 185
Levitt, Theodore, 161
Lexus, 146
Li, Charlene, 12, 132, 164
Lidl, 212
listening activities. *See* "themes and streams" component
Los Alamos National Laboratory, 84
loyalty cards and programs, 130, 212–13
Lyft, 27

M

Machiavelli, Niccolò, 17
Macpherson, Lisa, 96, 131–32, 135–36
Mangia, Karen, 131
Maor, Dana, 58
"marketing and communications as flow" component, 109, 111, 149–57
    addition of technology, 151–52
    customer preference, 154–55
    information as way to adjust dynamically, 153–54
    marketing as immediate and bidirectional channel, 154
    mindset and cultural development, 205–6
    relationship to other Digital Helix components, 143–44, 156, 191
    tests and experiments, 155–56
Marketo, 85, 151
McKinsey, 56, 65–66, 185
"Meaning Makers," 211
metrics, 95
    absence of reliable, 71
    "all together and one step ahead" component, 189
    concept shift to insights that drive decisions that matter, 95
    culture and, 196
    "customers' experiential portfolios" component, 145–46
    Seven Challenges to Digital Transformation, 55, 72–75
microfinancing, 40
Microsoft, x, 129
Miéville, China, 117
millennials, 37, 157
mindset and cultural development, 195–208
    "all for one and one for all" component and, 206
    "all together and one step ahead" component and, 207
    building high-performance culture, 197
    command of self, 198
    curiosity toward mastery, 198
    "customers' experiential portfolios" component and, 205
    empowering individuals into optimal mindset, 196–97
    "executives as explorers" component and, 204
    fatigue, 202–3
    filtering, 203
    learning to take risks, 199
    "marketing and communications as flow" component and, 205–6
    pressures than hinder performance, 201
    propensity for handling failure, 199
    questionnaire/audit regarding, 203–4

"sales as connected moments"
   component and, 206
taking risk and failure hand in hand,
   203
"themes and streams" component and,
   205
time as precious resource, 199–200
trainable mental skills, 200–202
MIT, 46, 189
mobile technology, 22–23, 37, 43, 77, 86,
   129
Moore, Geoffrey, 31
motivated blindness, 115

N

Nadella, Satya, x, 38–39
Netflix, 25, 129
Newell, Alien, 216
New York Police Department, 129
Nike, 19, 36
99Designs, 40
Nokia, 80
Nordstrom, 36

O

Observers, 60–61
Office365, x
Ogilvy, David, 96
Omniture, 11
O'Reilly, Tim, 172
Orwell, George, 209
outsourcing, 55, 78–79

P

P&G, 84
Pareto's law (80:20 rule), 212–13, 218
pattern recognition, 216
Patton, George S., Jr., 173–74
Peppers, Don, 160
pin theory, 14
Platt, Lew, 79
Polman, Paul, 124
Porter, Michael, 87
The Power of Noticing (Bazerman), 115,
   210

The Prince (Machiavelli), 17
programmed marketing responses, 214–15
PulsePoint Group, 52, 59, 90

Q

Qdoba Mexican Grill, 129–30
Quicken, 36
Quiznos, 80

R

Radian6, 122
recommendations, reviews, and ratings, 23,
   38, 138
Reich, Angelika, 58
retrofitting, 105–6, 152
Rogers, Bruce, 65, 76, 108
Rogers, Martha, 160
Rolex, 43
Rutherford, Linda, 46

S

"sales as connected moments" component,
   109, 111, 159–70
   aligning culture, 169–70
   building right systems, 169
   content slices, 162
   customer control, 162
   delivering for exact moments, 165–66
   identifying moments, 167–69
   mindset and cultural development, 206
   nonlinear model, 163
   old versus new sales model, 164–65
   questionnaire/audit regarding, 166–67
   relationship to other Digital Helix
      components, 143, 191
   successful relationships, 159–61
Salesforce, 11, 25, 68, 85, 122, 151, 164, 166
Samsung, 144
Samuelson, Paul, 34
SanDisk, 74–75
Satoro, Ryunosuke, 60
Schenkel, Gerd, 77–78
Schmidt, Eric, 84
Schrage, Michael, 2, 5, 11, 14–15, 24–25,
   105–6, 118, 138, 172, 187, 189–90,
   196, 215–18

Schumpeter, Joseph, xii
Schwartz, Mark, 14, 133
Scott, Larry, 119, 139
segmentation model, 59–61
Seven Challenges to Digital
　Transformation, 51–61, 63–87
　　architecture and collaboration, 54,
　　　75–78
　　audit regarding, 53, 64
　　avoiding, 60
　　common theme among, 86–87
　　core competency within, 55, 78–79
　　erroneous assumptions, 97–98
　　executive engagement, 52, 65–68
　　expectations chasm, 54, 69–72
　　learning from failures, 58–59
　　leveraging digital across business, 56,
　　　84–86
　　metrics, 55, 72–75
　　openness to alternative strategies,
　　　55–56, 79–84
　　segmentation model, 59–61
　　universal clarity regarding, 56–57
Seven Drivers of Digital Opportunity, 31,
　33–34
　　access to more information, 37–39
　　compression of supply and demand,
　　　34–36
　　exponential rate of change, 42–45
　　new digital competitors, 40–42
　　organizational audit regarding, 49–50
　　pay-as-you-go, 39–40
　　price, efficiency, and innovation trade-
　　　offs, 45–46
　　questionnaire/audit regarding, 47–48
　　shifting demographics, 36–37
"seven pressures" (Drucker), 32–33
SharePoint, 151
sickle cell anemia, 11
signal-to-noise ratios and filtering, 121,
　129–30, 136, 191, 203, 207, 210–11
silo orientation, 67, 172, 197
Silver, Nate, 125
Simon, Herbert A., 216
Smith, Adam, 11, 14, 34, 197
Snowden, Edward, 37
Social Media Accelerator, 12–13, 59
social media and technology, 12–13,
　22–23, 54–56, 59–60, 93, 106, 164–65
Solis, Brian, 63

Southwest Airlines, 45
Starbucks, 86, 130
startups, 41–42, 175, 199
steamships, 21, 26, 105, 152
Steinert, John, 150
Stop/Start/Do Differently method, 92,
　99–101
StubHub, 35
Subway, 80
Sull, Charles, 80, 184
Sull, Donald, 80, 184

T

Tag Heuer, 43
Tao of Physics: An Exploration of the
　Parallels Between Modern Physics and
　Eastern Mysticism (Capra), 52
Telstra, 77–78
Tesco, 212–13
Tesla, ix, 25, 40, 181
"themes and streams" component, 109–10,
　125–36
　　adjusting and adapting to change,
　　　125–26
　　bias toward the familiar, 126
　　defined, 127
　　discerning signal from noise, 129
　　filtering, 130, 134
　　illusion of control, 134
　　listening, 127, 130–31
　　living microscope, 128–30
　　mindset and cultural development, 205
　　"next best offers," 129
　　questionnaire/audit regarding, 131–33
　　relationship to other Digital Helix
　　　components, 156, 179, 191
　　variables driving success, 130
Thinking, Fast and Slow (Kahnemen), 115
Thrivers, 13, 60–61, 190
Tisch Center for Hospitality and Tourism,
　157
Toynbee, Arnold, 9
Toyota, 146
Trailblazers, 59, 61
Trend Spotting and Tracking Template,
　44–45
Twain, Mark, 59–61
Twitter, 23

U

Uber, ix, 25–27, 135, 207
UPS, 188
Urban, Tim, xi

V

"The Value of Signal (and the Cost of Noise)" (Cognizant), 211

W

Walmart, ix, 181
Watson, James D., xii, 105
wearable devices, 23, 43
Web 1.0, viii, 18, 39, 69
Web 2.0, viii, 18, 93

WebEx, 151
Welch, Jack, ix–x, 42, 195
What You See Is All There Is (WYSIATI), 116
Whole Foods, 14
WikiLeaks, 37
Winton, Jeff, 151

Y

Yelp, 138
YouTube, 23, 81

Z

Zappos, 41, 160, 186
Zoox, 27
Zuckerberg, Mark, 197

ABOUT THE AUTHORS

MICHAEL GALE founded Strategic Oxygen in 2001, which was widely seen as one of the technology industry's primary data toolsets for marketers, used by over 20 brands and used to model over $4 billion in marketing and sales investments. The company was sold to Monitor Group, where he was a group partner from 2006 to 2010. In 2011, he became a partner at Pulsepoint Group, a digital consulting company, which was acquired by ICF in 2015. Michael has also served as chief web officer and GM at Micron Technology and was the vice president of Worldwide brand research at IntelliQuest.

CHRIS AARONS has helped launch dozens of companies and products using a unique mix of digital, sales, and marketing strategies. At Pulsepoint Group, Chris helped leading organizations become digital in both their practice and delivery. In 2006, he launched one of the first social media departments at AMD and later wrote the book *Social Media Judo: The Essential Guide to Mastering Social Media and Delivering Real Results*. Chris also teaches digital marketing at the University of Texas at Austin and has won numerous awards for his digital programs while working for clients such as Adobe, Amazon, AMD, Cisco, Dell, HP, LG, Microsoft, Philips, and others.